BARRON'S

NEW JERSEY

GRADE 5

ELA/LITERACY TEST

Mark Riccardi, M.Ed.
Teacher, Language Arts
Crossroads North Middle School
South Brunswick, New Jersey

Kimberly Perillo, M.Ed.
Teacher, Instructional Support Language Arts
Crossroads North Middle School
South Brunswick, New Jersey

About the Authors

Mark Riccardi has been a language arts teacher in a middle school in South Brunswick, New Jersey, for the past 15 years. He received his BA in English Education from Trenton State College, now TCNJ, and his Masters in Educational Leadership from Seton Hall University. He lives with his wife, April, and two sons, Connor and Cameron, in Ocean County.

Kimberly Perillo is a middle school reading specialist in South Brunswick, New Jersey. She is a graduate of Trenton State College, now TCNJ, and has a master's degree in reading from Rutgers University. She has been a teacher trainer in reading strategies since 2005 and loves helping children understand challenging texts. She lives with her husband, John, and two children, Abigail and Robert, in Mercer County.

All inquiries should be addressed to:
Barron's Educational Series, Inc.
250 Wireless Boulevard
Hauppauge, NY 11788
www.barronseduc.com

ISBN: 978-1-4380-0560-7

Library of Congress Control Number: 2014957775

Manufactured by: B11R11
Date of manufacture: January 2015

Printed in the United States of America

9 8 7 6 5 4 3 2 1

Contents

Introduction—Meet the Test

Congratulations! You are on your way to achieving your best possible score on the PARCC English Language Arts test for Grade 5. By using all of the lessons, hints, and tips in this book, you should be able to earn your best score. Before we begin, read through the information on the next few pages. Hopefully this information will answer any questions you might have about the test.

What Is the PARCC?

The PARCC is the Partnership for Assessment of Readiness for College and Careers. This test will be a common assessment to every public school student in New Jersey as well as several other states in the country. The goal is to further develop college and career readiness for every student. Each year students are tested in English Language Arts (ELA) and Math. With the PARCC, testing will happen at least twice a year. The focus of this book will be on the English Language Arts section for fifth-grade students. The book will integrate the necessary skills to prepare students for both the Performance-Based Assessment (PBA), which is taken after 70 percent of the school year has been completed, and the End-of-Year Assessment (EOY), which is taken after 90 percent of the year has been completed.

What Will Be Required on Each Test (Performance-Based Assessment and End-of-Year Assessment)?

The PBA will include three parts: a literary analysis task, a narrative writing task, and a research simulation task. The Literary Analysis Task will require students to read literature, answer questions, and construct a literary analysis in response to two texts. The Narrative Task will require students to read a narrative passage and then construct a narrative piece of writing. According to PARCC, this can be a story, an historical account, or a description of an event, scene, or object. The Research Simulation Task will require students to read or view multiple texts to analyze information and construct analytical evidence-based essays.

The EOY exam will require students to read literature and informative texts and answer multiple-choice or technology-enhanced constructed-response questions.

This means students will have to respond to a question that is not multiple-choice. The student may have to click and drag information or highlight evidence. These types of questions will be evident throughout the practice book in a written format.

Why Do I Need to Take This Test?

Every public school student in the state of New Jersey takes this test. The state can then see that every student is able to complete tasks that are equal to their grade level. Your school can use the results of the test to make sure students are receiving the right programs and help any students who are struggling.

How Will This Book Help?

This book will help you prepare to take every part of the PARCC ELA Grade Five test. You should be well prepared for this test if you attend school every day and always do your best. The test is meant to test what every fifth-grade student should know. The book will set up test-like situations, so when you take the real test you will be comfortable. The more practice you have, the better you will do. Please note, the actual PARCC test will be administered on a computer. Students will need to type responses and understand basic computer operating procedures.

What Will This Book Cover?

This book will cover all elements of the PARCC test along with some basic skills necessary for good reading and writing. This book includes tips and practice for reading and writing narrative and expository text. On the test, students will be required to answer multiple-choice questions, manipulate textual evidence, and construct written responses. This book will explain each of these parts and provide tips, hints, and structures to make the PARCC test easier.

What Kind of Writing Will I Do?

On the PARCC, you will need to complete a variety of writing tasks. In this book, we will show you how to write both narrative and expository responses.

What Else Can I Do to Get Ready?

After using the tips and techniques in this book, the rest is up to you. The best way to prepare for this test is to do your best everyday. Pay attention in school, do all of your work, and always do your best. During the weeks of the PARCC, make sure you get plenty of rest every night, eat a good breakfast, and bring a positive attitude. With a lot of preparation and the right attitude, you can accomplish anything.

If I Complete This Book, Will I Be Guaranteed to Pass the Test?

Unfortunately, we cannot guarantee doing the work in this book will guarantee that you pass the test. The book will put you in the best possible position for success. If any section is difficult for you, make sure you go back over it again and take notes. Ask a parent or teacher to help you check work that you find difficult. Work hard and do your best. That is all you can ask of yourself. Now let's get going and prepare for the PARCC!

IMPORTANT NOTE: Barron's has made every effort to ensure that the content of this book is accurate as of press time, but the PARCC Assessments are constantly changing. Be sure to consult *www.parcconline.org* for all the latest testing information and scoring rubrics. Regardless of the changes being announced after press time, this book will still provide a strong framework for fifth-grade students preparing for the assessments.

Reading Informational Text

CHAPTER 1

Use the checklist to keep track of your work in this chapter.

- [ ] What Is Informational Text?
- [ ] Reading for Understanding
- [ ] Interacting with Text
- [ ] Understanding Expository Text Structure
- [ ] Central Idea
- [ ] Answering Multiple-Choice and Technology-Enhanced Constructed-Response Questions
- [ ] Practice Time!

What Is Informational Text?

Think about the text you encounter on a daily basis. What do you see? You might read novels or stories, which would be narrative text or literature. You might also see newspapers, magazine articles, textbooks, letters, or directions. These are all examples of informational text. This type of text is meant to provide information to the reader and may persuade, provide an argument, or explain procedures.

Throughout the PARCC, you will see informational text. For the Performance-Based Assessment (Part 1 of the PARCC), you will see this in the Research Task where you will answer questions and write an essay. On the End-of-Year Assessment (Part 2 of the PARCC), you will read articles and answer different kinds of questions.

Reading for Understanding

As you read informational text, it is really important to use strategies as you read to help you understand and remember the text. You will have limited time for each part of the test, and you don't want to waste time rereading. Your goal is to **read and understand the first time**! This happens when you take your time and use your reading strategies.

Now, you might be tempted to look ahead and read the multiple-choice questions first, but you should not do this! You might be asking, "Why not?" Perhaps you've even had someone tell you this is a good strategy to use. If you read the questions ahead of time, you probably will not focus on all of the details of the story, and guess what? You will need ALL of the details of the article to answer the questions or construct an essay. More important, you are wasting precious time reading questions and answers that you probably won't remember later when reading the text. The only question you SHOULD read is the prose constructed response (PCR) question. This is where you will be writing an essay. Reading this question, will allow you to identify and mark evidence as you read, which will save you time on the writing task. On the PARCC, you will read on the computer and have electronic highlighters available. Use these to mark key ideas or possible evidence for the essay.

Now, how can you accomplish your goal of doing well on this part of the test? You will need to apply reading strategies and interact with the text. This may slow your reading slightly, but it will be well worth it if you don't have to go back later and reread for every question on the test. Each time you use a strategy to interact with the text, you are sending a message to your brain that this is important information and should be remembered. These strategies are done in your head, but you can also use those highlighters!

Take a few minutes to review the reading strategies below.

READING STRATEGIES

- **Predict:** Guess what will happen in the text.
- **Question:** Ask questions of the author and text.
- **Connect:** Make connections between the article and other text, the world, or your life.
- **Visualize:** Picture what is happening in your head.
- **Summarize:** Stop periodically and retell what has happened so far in the story.
- **Infer:** Look for the clues, think about what you already know and make a guess or draw a conclusion.
- **Use Context Clues:** If you don't know a word, use the words around it to try and figure it out. Check if the author provided an example, synonym or antonym to help you figure out the definition.

Let's give it a try. We're going to read two paragraphs from an article and interact with the text. You will see my thoughts in parenthesis. Afterward, you will have a chance to practice!

School Lunches: Are They Healthy?

Cafeteria lunches have gotten a bad rap for years. *(The cafeteria lunches aren't very good in my school.)* Although people imagine the typical lunch lady, wearing a hair net and plopping unrecognizable food onto every child's tray, this is luckily not the case in many school cafeterias today. *(I've seen this in movies, but our lunch ladies don't look like this.)* Now, with new federal health regulations developed by the United States Department of Agriculture, food has become healthier and in some cases better. *(What does regulations mean? The regulations make it healthier, so it's something they have to do, like a rule.)* Yet, there is still debate among students about whether these new regulations are fair and parents about whether these rules work. Students feel they are old enough to make their own food choices and don't agree with the government mandating the food they eat. Yet, they are dumping most of the healthy foods into the garbage cans. *(If there are rules, why aren't they eating healthier meals?)* This is a growing problem across the country. *(Sounds like the article is going to talk about the problem of unhealthy lunches for kids.)*

What was going through your head as you read? Write down questions, connections, or any other thoughts that popped into your head as you read the paragraph.

What strategies did you see used in the sample?

- [x] **Predict:** The reader predicted what the article would be about.
- [x] **Question:** The reader questioned why kids aren't eating healthier if there are rules.
- [x] **Connect:** The reader connected to the cafeteria in her own school as well as movies she's seen with lunch ladies.
- [ ] **Visualize:** The author may have visualized in his or her head but we cannot see it in the text.
- [ ] **Summarize:** The author did not summarize.
- [ ] **Infer:** Look for the clues, think about what you already know, and make a guess or draw a conclusion.
- [x] **Use Context Clues:** The author used context clues to figure out the word regulation.

The author should have visualized, but this is done in your brain. As you read, picture what you are reading in your head. Again, this tells your brain it's important and to remember it.

In addition, the author did not summarize, but we know this is a really important strategy to use when reading this type of text. How can we summarize this paragraph? Let's read it one more time and look for key words. Then, we'll try to rewrite the paragraph in just a sentence or two.

School Lunches: Are They Healthy?

Cafeteria lunches have gotten a bad rap for years. Although people imagine the typical lunch lady, wearing a hair net and plopping unrecognizable food onto every child's tray, this is luckily not the case in many school cafeterias today. Now, with new federal health regulations developed by the United States Department of Agriculture, food has become healthier and in some cases better. Yet, there is still debate among students about whether these new laws are fair and parents about whether these rules work. Students feel they are old enough to make their own food choices and don't agree with the government mandating the food they eat. Yet, they are dumping most of the healthy foods into the garbage cans. This is a growing problem across the country.

Let's take these ideas and put them into one or two sentences.

Although the federal government regulates the food served in school cafeterias, it is unclear whether the regulations are helping kids eat healthier.

Interacting with Text

It's your turn to give it a try. Read another paragraph from the article. Remember to stop yourself and interact with the text. Ask questions, make connections, react to the text, and summarize. When you are finished, try to write a one- or two-sentence summary of the paragraph. Your goal is to train yourself to do these things as you read. By using these strategies, you will understand and remember more of the text. Write on the text if it helps you.

When students step into the cafeteria line they are offered a well-balanced meal. A complete lunch comprises food from every food group. Unfortunately, this is not the choice most students make. Instead of chicken, rice, beans, fruit, and skim milk, many trays have multiple packs of baked chips and low fat cookies. Is this a healthier choice? Too many of these lighter versions are still unhealthy for kids. Likewise, many students who buy the complete lunch quickly take their tray to the garbage and remove the fruits and vegetables before sitting at the table. Children need nutrient-rich foods to help their developing bodies grow.

What strategies did you use as you read this paragraph?

- [ ] **Predict:** Guess what will happen in the text.
- [ ] **Question:** Ask questions of the author and text.
- [ ] **Connect:** Make connections between the text and your life, other text, or the world.
- [ ] **Visualize:** Picture what is happening in your head.

- [ ] **Summarize:** Stop periodically and retell what has happened so far in the article.
- [ ] **Infer:** Look for the clues, think about what you already know, and make a guess or draw a conclusion.
- [ ] **Use Context Clues:** If you don't know a word, use the words around it to try and figure it out.

How did you summarize this paragraph? Write one or two sentences to explain what this paragraph is about.

Answers are on page 149.

Understanding Expository Text Structure

Most of the time everyday text, or informational text, follows a basic three-part structure. The first part is the introduction, which is typically the first paragraph of the text. Here the author grabs the reader's attention and lets the reader know what to expect in the article, essay, letter, or other text. The second part of the structure is the body of the text. This is the biggest part of the writing and the place where the reader will gather the most information. This is where the author will explain, inform, or persuade the reader by using evidence and examples to support his or her point. Finally, the author will conclude his or her writing. This is usually the last paragraph of the text. The author will remind the reader of the point of the writing and leave the reader with something to think about.

Within this basic structure, the author will vary the organization depending on his or her purpose. Often you will be asked to identify the text structure. This means you need to examine the author's purpose and determine how the text is organized. You will be able to look for signal words to help figure out the structure. Below are four common structures seen in expository writing.

Structure	Definition	Signal Words
Sequential	The text will tell an order of events or step-by-step directions.	First, Next, Then
Compare and Contrast	The text will show similarities and differences.	Similar, Likewise, However, In contrast, Both, Different
Cause and Effect	The text will explain the results of an action. There may be more than one cause or more than one effect.	As a result, Since, Because, The effect of, The cause
Problem and Solution	The text will describe a problem and give one or more solutions.	This solves, One reason, The answer

Let's Practice

Read each short passage and identify the text structure. As you read, look for signal words to help you identify the structure.

1. This year Wick Middle School is struggling to update the technology available within the school. Students are being required to develop technology skills, yet the computers are outdated. As a result, seventh and eighth graders in Wick Township are falling behind the surrounding schools. Students do not know how to complete simple tasks, such as building a database and creating a powerpoint. In the end, students will be at a disadvantage in the job market.

Structure: ____

2. This year Wick Middle School is struggling to update the technology available within the school. Students are being required to develop technology skills, yet the computers are outdated. As a result, students decided to raise money. Some students are campaigning for a community spaghetti dinner fundraiser. Students will sell tickets to a dinner where they will cook and serve. Another idea is to ask businesses in the community to sponsor a grade by purchasing a tablet. The hope is to create a set of tablets for classes to rotate throughout the building.

Structure: ____

3. This year Wick Middle School is struggling to update the technology available within the school. Students are being required to develop technology skills, yet the computers are outdated. In September, school administrators inventoried the technology in the building and surveyed students and teachers about their technology knowledge. A few months later, school leaders met with parents to discuss funding the much needed technology need. Then, in March a fundraising campaign was implemented. This resulted in the purchase of 100 new tablets in early June. Next year, the group will continue fundraising efforts.

   Structure: ____________________

4. This year Wick Middle School is struggling to update the technology available within the school. Students are being required to develop technology skills, yet the computers are outdated. In contrast, neighboring Brun Middle School has computers in every classroom. Although the two towns are very similar economically, students at Brun are completing virtual labs in science, while students at Wick are still using textbooks and listening to the teacher lecture. Brun kids are collaborating on projects through technology, while Wick students are working independently. This difference puts Wick students at a real disadvantage.

   Structure: ____________________

Answers are on page 149.

Central Idea

The central idea is very important to this type of writing. It is often found in the first paragraph and tells the reader what the text will be about. Sometimes it is implied, and the reader needs to figure it out based on the details of the story. This means the author doesn't come right out and tell the reader but instead gives clues in order for the reader to figure out the topic of the writing.

Let's Practice

We're going to look at a few examples to identify the central idea. Read each paragraph below. Then try to figure out the central idea. Ask yourself, what is the topic or subject of the text? What does the author want me to know about this topic or subject? Look at the details for help.

Paragraph 1

Many people claim that dog is man's best friend. Over time, dogs have helped people find food and protect their homes. Most important, dogs are companions for many people. Yet, others will argue that dogs can be dangerous, are expensive, and are lots of work. These people will say if you are looking for good company, then you are looking for a cat. Cats are easy to take care of and reliable. However, many people are allergic to cats and they can scratch your furniture. As you decide the best pet for you and your family, you will need to weigh the positives and negatives of owning either a dog or a cat.

1. What is the central idea of the article? Ask yourself, what is the topic and what does the author want me to know about this topic? Write only one sentence.

---

2. What is the organization of the text?

- [ ] Sequential
- [ ] Compare and contrast
- [ ] Cause and effect
- [ ] Problem and solution

3. How do you know this is the structure?

Paragraph 2

Reed Johnson sits wheezing in his favorite chair watching television. He has been out of work for the past six months because of lung cancer, and his family can barely afford to pay the monthly bills. Reed started smoking as a teenager, and now 20 years later he is paying the price. Although the number of teens who smoke has recently decreased, it is still a prevalent problem in America. In 2008, 1 in 8 high school seniors were smoking cigarettes. This is still way too high, considering the research on the effects of smoking.

1. What is the central idea of the article? Ask yourself, what is the topic and what does the author want me to know about this topic? Write only one sentence.

---

2. What is the organization of the text?

- [ ] Sequential
- [ ] Compare and contrast
- [ ] Cause and effect
- [ ] Problem and solution

3. How do you know this is the structure?

Answers are on page 149.

Answering Multiple-Choice and Technology-Enhanced Constructed-Response Questions

After reading the text, you will answer multiple-choice questions and technology-enhanced constructed-response questions. Technology-enhanced questions may ask you to drag and drop information into a chart, highlight information, or construct a table. For this type of question, you will have to move or manipulate text in some way. When you take the PARCC, you will be on a computer. For this book, you will see questions with this structure, but you will use your pencil to answer. Take a minute to review the following hints.

HINTS FOR MULTIPLE-CHOICE QUESTIONS

- Identify key words in both the questions and answers. Make sure you understand what the question is asking you to do for the test.
- Read the entire question and ALL of the answer choices. If more than one answer seems correct, check to see if there is an option for "all of the above." If not, then choose the BEST answer.
- Don't get tricked when you see choices right from the text. Sometimes when an answer looks familiar, kids will choose it, but it might not answer the question. Make sure you read carefully and know what the question is asking.
- Use the process of elimination. Cross off answers that you know are incorrect.
- Answer EVERY question. Make a logical guess if you don't know the answer.
- Don't try to be the first to finish! When you are done, check over your answers carefully.

Let's Practice

Read the complete article "School Lunches: Are They Healthy?" and apply your reading strategies. Remember, you can write on the text. Then answer the multiple-choice questions. When you are finished, check your answers at the end of the book.

School Lunches: Are They Healthy?

by Kim Perillo

Cafeteria lunches have gotten a bad rap for years. Although people imagine the typical lunch lady, wearing a hair net and plopping unrecognizable food onto every child's tray, this is luckily not the case in many school cafeterias today. Now, with new federal health regulations developed by the United States Department of Agriculture, food has become healthier and in some cases better. Yet, there is still debate among students about whether these new laws are fair and parents about whether these rules work. Students feel they are old enough to make their own food choices and don't agree with the government mandating the food they eat. Yet, they are dumping most of the healthy foods into the garbage cans. This is a growing problem across the country.

While students miss real potato chips, greasy French fries, and sugary drinks, parents are disappointed to find out their children are not eating the fruit and vegetables being offered. State and federal regulations do not matter if students are not eating the food. As a result, it is time to evaluate the food being served in school cafeterias and possibly change the implementation of these new rules, in order to increase the consumption of fruits and vegetables during the school day.

When students step into the cafeteria line they are offered a well-balanced meal. A complete lunch comprises food from every food group. Unfortunately, this is not the choice most students make. Instead of chicken, rice, beans, fruit, and skim milk, many trays have multiple packs of baked chips and low fat cookies. Is this a healthier choice? Too much of these lighter versions is still unhealthy for kids.

Likewise, many students who buy the complete lunch quickly take their tray to the garbage and remove the fruits and vegetables before sitting at the table. Children need nutrient rich foods to help their developing bodies grow.

Unfortunately, many parents are unaware of the food being eaten by their children at school. They assume their son or daughter is eating a healthy, well-balanced meal. Samantha, a fifth grader, reported eating pizza and chips every day for lunch. When asked about the complete lunch offered, including fruit and vegetable, she replied, "No one eats that! I don't know why they even offer it."

Even more concerning, childhood obesity is on the rise, and children aren't taking control of the problem themselves. According to the Center for Disease Control, close to 18 percent of children between the ages of 6 and 11 are obese and approximately one third of children are either overweight or obese. Therefore, adults need to intervene and help solve this problem. Furthermore, seventy percent of these obese children have at least one risk factor for heart disease. Consequently, there is no time to wait. Changes need to happen immediately.

There are many possible solutions for improving school lunches. Perhaps it's time to have more involvement with the students themselves. If children play a part in healthy menu planning, they will be more likely to eat what is on their tray. Alex, an upper elementary student, said, "At home, I go to the grocery store with my mom and I get to pick the fruits and vegetables we're going to eat for the week. I eat more vegetables at home because we buy the things I like, and they taste better." This may be a simple solution, as long as the vegetables taste good. Parents need to ban together and insist on fresh produce for their kids rather than canned products.

According to the United States Department of Agriculture, "School meals must look and taste good if children are going to eat them. To address this need, we have developed and distributed a wide range of materials designed to provide local meal planners with recipes and other tools to help them prepare appealing meals." Local districts must take advantage of the resources provided and begin transforming current meals into healthy and delicious meals that children will want to eat when they sit down at lunch.

At some elementary schools, half of the students go to recess before lunch, while the other half goes after lunch. The school reports, "Students going to recess before lunch, eat more and waste less than kids going to recess after lunch." If kids exercise and play before lunch, they will be hungry, and eat more of the healthy foods on their tray. This is a quick and easy solution to improve healthy eating.

Changes are happening in school cafeterias, but they will not be successful without the support of kids and adults. Perhaps parents, teachers, and school administrators need to think further about how to help kids make the right choices. Healthy eating should not be forced, but instead needs to become the norm for every child.

1. **Part A.** In paragraph 1 it says, "Now, with new federal health regulations developed by the United States Department of Agriculture, food has become healthier and in some cases better." What is a regulation?

 - ○ a. Free choice
 - ○ b. Keeping food fresh
 - ○ c. Punishment
 - ○ d. Law or rule

Part B. Reread the following excerpt. Underline two sentences that help you understand the meaning of regulations.

Cafeteria lunches have gotten a bad rap for years. Although people imagine the typical lunch lady, wearing a hair net and plopping unrecognizable food onto every kid's tray, this is luckily not the case in many school cafeterias today. Now, with new federal health regulations developed by the United States Department of Agriculture, food has become healthier and in some cases better. Yet, there is still debate among students about whether these new laws are fair and parents about whether these rules work. Students feel they are old enough to make their own food choices and don't agree with the government mandating the food they eat. Yet, they are dumping most of the healthy foods into the garbage cans. This is a growing problem across the country.

2. Part A. What is the text structure of "School Lunches: Are They Healthy?"

○ a. Compare and contrast

○ b. Sequential

○ c. Cause and effect

○ d. Problem and solution

Part B. Which two details provide evidence for your choice in Part A?

☐ a. *This is a growing problem across the country.*

☐ b. *A complete lunch comprises food from every food group.*

☐ c. *These children are at a greater risk for heart disease, and diabetes later in life.*

☐ d. *There is still debate among students about whether these new regulations are fair.*

☐ e. *There are many possible solutions for improving school lunches.*

3. Circle the sentence that best represents the main idea of the article. Then, draw a line to connect the main idea to two supporting details.

MAIN IDEAS	SUPPORTING DETAILS
Schools should be the only ones controlling school lunches.	Childhood obesity has more than doubled over the past three years.
It's time to examine cafeteria food regulations and find a way to increase the amounts of fruits and vegetables eaten.	The school reports, "Students going to recess before lunch, eat more and waste less than kids going to recess after lunch."
New cafeteria regulations are working just fine.	Many parents are unaware of the food being eaten by their children at school.
There should be no regulations because kids can make their own food choices.	When kids step into the cafeteria line they are offered a well-balanced meal.
Parents should be in control of what their kids eat.	I eat more vegetables at home because we buy the things I like, and they taste better." This may be a simple solution, as long as the vegetables taste good.

Answers are on page 149.

Practice Time!

Now it is your turn to practice on your own. On the following pages, you will read an informational text and answer questions. Good luck and remember to use all of the hints you learned! When you are finished, check your answers in the back of the book. When you take the PARCC, it is possible for you to see one longer text, such as this practice, or two shorter passages.

Video Games: Helping or Hurting Kids Today

1 According to CNN Health, approximately 90 percent of kids between the ages of 8 and 16 spend approximately 13 hours a week playing video games. This excessive amount of time spent in front of a gaming system causes concern among many parents. Adults fear their children will become more violent because of the video games they play. Some parents forbid their children from playing certain games and others want state legislature to pass laws further regulating video games. Contrary, there are some benefits to children playing video games. Not only can they teach logic and problem solving skills, they also teach kids how to follow directions. Therefore, the question remains do the benefits of video games outweigh the dangers?

2 Most kids will argue that video games are fun and worth playing. The overall opinion of American youth is that they will not make kids violent. Cameron, a fifth grader in South Bound Brook, claims that all of his friends play video games and it doesn't make them angry or aggressive. "Movies might influence kids to do bad things, but everyone knows video games are just for fun." However, recent studies published by the *American Pediatric Journal* found both American and Japanese children who play violent video games show greater signs of aggression. The study compared the number of hours spent playing violent video games to aggressive behaviors, which included hitting, kicking, and fighting other kids. The study proved that younger children were more influenced than older kids by video games.

3 Angelo, a fifth grader in Hamilton Township, agrees with the findings. "Sometimes kids in school fight with each other and they use moves from video games. They think they can beat anyone just because they are good at a game." This mentality in today's youth is the cause of concern for many adults.

4 One solution to keep young children safe was to rate video games. If a video game is rated M for mature, stores cannot sell it to minors. Unfortunately, this doesn't always keep young children from playing the games. Older siblings, relatives, and sometimes, even parents allow children to watch and play these aggressive games. More than 85% of all parents do not actually monitor the rating of video games. In order for society to have less violent children, parents need to monitor kids and make sure they are playing appropriate games. Appropriate games can offer valuable learning for today's youth. James Gee, a professor of learning sciences at the University of Wisconsin, found that video games actually boost brainpower. Gee claims, "We had a hard time finding kids who were bad at school but good at games."

5 Additionally, exercise can be a benefit of video games today. The Nintendo Wii allows for people to physically take part in games. With this console, participants box, play tennis, bowl, and much more. Although the activity is not equivalent to actively taking part in the real life sport, it certainly is better than sitting around watching TV or playing a more sedentary game.

6 In the end, parents need to find a way for kids to benefit from the positive aspects of gaming without becoming overly aggressive. With proper supervision and support from adults and responsibility from children it is possible to accomplish both. The goal is to maximize the technology available today while keeping kids safe.

1. **Part A.** The article talks frequently about aggression. What is the best definition of aggression?

- ○ a. Deliberately, unfriendly behavior
- ○ b. Playing video games
- ○ c. Acting as a loner
- ○ d. Rating video games

Part B. Which two details from the article best support your answer to Part A?

- ☐ a. *Recent studies published by the* American Pediatric Journal *found both American and Japanese children who play violent video games show greater signs of aggression.*
- ☐ b. *This mentality in today's youth is the cause of concern for many adults.*
- ☐ c. *The Nintendo Wii allows for people to physically take part in games.*
- ☐ d. *The study compared the number of hours spent playing violent video games to aggressive behaviors, which included hitting, kicking, and fighting other kids.*
- ☐ e. *One solution to keep young children safe was to rate video games.*
- ☐ f. *Cameron, a fifth grader in South Bound Brook, claims that all of his friends play video games and it doesn't make them angry or aggressive.*

2. Use the listed idea to best complete the diagram. Fill in two pros (benefits of video games), two cons (negatives of video games), and a conclusion drawn from the article.

IDEA BANK

13 hours a week playing video games	Boosts brainpower	Kids mimic fighting behaviors	Leads to more aggressive behaviors
Video game ratings	Movies influence negative behaviors	Parents need to closely monitor video game use	Movement and exercise opportunities

VIDEO GAMES

PROS	CONS
CONCLUSION	

3. **Part A.** How did the author support the idea that game ratings are not always effective in protecting children from inappropriate games?

- ○ a. The author tells a story, or anecdote.
- ○ b. The author provides statistical evidence.
- ○ c. The author quotes an expert.
- ○ d. James Gee, a professor of learning sciences at the University of Wisconsin, found that video games actually boost brainpower.

Part B. Which detail best supports the answer to Part A?

- ○ a. *Stores cannot sell it to minors.*
- ○ b. *Older siblings, relatives, and sometimes, even parents allow children to watch and play these aggressive games.*
- ○ c. *More than 85% of all parents do not actually monitor the rating of video games.*
- ○ d. *One solution to keep young children safe was to rate video games.*

4. **Part A.** Professor Gee claims, "We had a hard time finding kids who were bad at school but good at games." What conclusion can you draw from this statement?

- ○ a. Kids who play video games learn how to think and do well in school.
- ○ b. Kids who play video games don't do their homework.
- ○ c. Kids who play video games are loners.
- ○ d. Kids who play video games do poorly in school.

Part B. Which detail is most substantial in proving your answer for Part A?

- ○ a. *Nintendo Wii allows for people to physically take part in games.*
- ○ b. *Adults fear their children will become more violent.*
- ○ c. *Some parents forbid their children from playing certain games.*
- ○ d. *Video games actually boost brainpower.*

Answers are on page 151.

References

Anderson, Craig A., and Dill, Karen, E. (2000). Video games and aggressive thoughts, feelings, and behavior in the laboratory and in life. *Journal of Personality and Social Psychology*, 78, 4, 772–790.

Bakalar, Nicholas (2008, January 1). "Exercise: Better than the couch, but not equal to the court." *New York Times*. (*http://www.nytimes.com/2008/01/01/health/nutrition/01exer.html*)

"Childhood Obesity Facts." Centers for Disease Control and Prevention, 27 Feb. 2014. (*http://www.cdc.gov/healthyyouth/obesity/facts.htm*)

Gentile, Douglas A., Lynch, Paul J., Linder, Jennifer R., and Walsh, David (2004). The effects of violent video game habits on adolescent hostility, aggressive behaviors, and school performance. *Journal of Adolescence*, 27, 5–22.

Johnson, Steven (2005, July 24). Your brain on video games: Could they actually be good for you? *Discover Magazine*. (*http://www.discovermagazine.com/2005/jul/brain-on-video-games*)

"School Meals." *USDA School Meals FAQ*. United States Department of Agriculture, 16 Dec. 2013. (*http://www.fns.usda.gov/school-meals/faqs*)

CHAPTER 2

Research Task

Use the checklist to keep track of your work in this chapter.

- [ ] What Is the Research Task?
- [ ] Begin at the Beginning
- [ ] Prewriting
- [ ] Writing a Thesis Statement
- [ ] Interest Catcher
- [ ] Body Paragraphs and Supporting Details
- [ ] Conclusion
- [ ] Hints for Success
- [ ] Transitions
- [ ] Word Choice
- [ ] Sentence Structure
- [ ] Practice Time!

What Is the Research Task?

One task you will have to complete on the PARCC is the research task. Even if you do not have experience with this, you do not need to worry. You already have experience with all of the skills you need for this part of the test. You will be reading two or three nonfiction texts and then constructing an essay. When you take the PARCC, one of your texts may be a video. You will watch the video and gather evidence, just as you do for a written article.

You have already learned about reading informational text in Chapter 1. For this part of the test, you will need to use these strategies. You want to read each text carefully in order to complete the questions and writing assignment. After researching, or reading multiple texts about a topic, you will plan, write, and edit an essay. Do not worry if this task sounds difficult. If you follow and practice the steps in this chapter, you will have no problem completing the task to the best of your ability.

This chapter will break the essay down into its most basic parts: identifying your evidence, prewriting, introduction, body of the essay, and conclusion. Once you have mastered each part, you will have the opportunity to put it all together. Ready? Let's get started!

Begin at the Beginning

It can be said that your score on the research task will be decided in the first five minutes of the test. Does this sound crazy? It might, but your first two choices could decide how well you do on this part of the test. The first part will be to read the text and prompt carefully. Remember, use your strategies and highlight your test, when necessary. After you read each text, you will answer a few questions. Then you will face the writing prompt. As you read the prompt, underline the part of the prompt that asks you the question. The prompt will contain all of the background information you will need to begin writing, but they will only ask you one question. Make sure you know what is being asked of you.

Let's look back at our first text from Chapter 1. You already read this and answered questions. Reread the first text. Then, read the passages that follow and answer the questions. Use all of the strategies and tips learned in Chapter 1.

Today you will research healthy eating in schools. You will read two articles and view a sample menu from the U.S. Department of Agriculture. As you read, you will gather information and answer questions in order to write an essay.

Text 1

School Lunches: Are They Healthy?

by Kim Perillo

1 Cafeteria lunches have gotten a bad rap for years. Although people imagine the typical lunch lady, wearing a hair net and plopping unrecognizable food onto every child's tray, this is luckily not the case in many school cafeterias today. Now, with new health regulations, food has become healthier and in some cases better. Yet, there is still debate among students about whether these new regulations are fair and parents about whether these rules work. Students feel they are old enough to make their own food choices and don't agree with the government mandating the food they eat. Yet, they are dumping most of the healthy foods into the garbage cans. This is a growing problem across the country.

2 While the kids miss real potato chips, greasy French fries, and sugary drinks, parents are disappointed to find out their kids are not eating the fruit and vegetables being offered. State and federal regulations do not matter if students are not eating the food. As a result, it is time to evaluate the food being served in school cafeterias and possibly change the implementation of these new rules, in order to increase the consumption of fruits and vegetables during the school day.

3 When students step into the cafeteria line they are offered a well-balanced meal. A complete lunch comprises food from every food group. Unfortunately, this is not the choice most students make. Instead of chicken, rice, beans, fruit, and skim milk, many trays have multiple packs of baked chips and low fat cookies. Is this a healthier choice for kids? Too much of these lighter versions is still unhealthy for kids. Likewise, many students who buy the complete lunch quickly take their tray to the garbage and remove the fruits and vegetables before sitting at the table. Children need nutrient rich foods to help their developing bodies grow.

4 Unfortunately, many parents are unaware of the food being eaten by their children at school. They assume their son or daughter is eating a healthy, well-balanced meal. Samantha, a fifth grader, reported eating pizza and chips every day for lunch. When asked about the complete lunch offered, including fruit and vegetable, she replied, "No one eats that! I don't know why they even offer it."

5 Even more concerning, childhood obesity is on the rise and kids aren't taking control of the problem themselves. According to the Center for Disease Control, close to 18 percent of children between the ages of 6 and 11 are obese and approximately one-third of children are either overweight or obese. Furthermore, seventy percent of these obese children will become obese adults and these children are at a greater risk for heart disease, and diabetes later in life. Consequently, there is no time to wait. Changes need to happen immediately.

6 There are many possible solutions for improving school lunches. Perhaps it's time to have more involvement with the students themselves. If children play a part in healthy menu planning, they will be more likely to eat what is on their tray. Alex, an upper elementary student, said, "At home, I go to the grocery store with my mom and I get to pick the fruits and vegetables we're going to eat for the week. I eat more vegetables at home because we buy the things I like, and they taste better." This may be a simple solution, as long as the vegetables taste good. Parents need to ban together and insist on fresh produce for their kids rather than canned products.

7 At some elementary schools, half of the students go to recess before lunch, while the other half goes after lunch. The school reports, "Kids going to recess before lunch, eat more and waste less than kids going to recess after lunch." If kids exercise and play before lunch, they will be hungry, and eat more of the healthy foods on their tray. This is a quick and easy solution to improve healthy eating.

8 Changes are happening in school cafeterias, but they will not be successful without the support of kids and adults. Perhaps parents, teachers, and school administrators need to think further about how to help kids make the right choices. Healthy eating should not be forced, but instead needs to become the norm for every child.

You have already answered the questions for this text, so let's go right to the next article, which is an excerpt from: USDA (U.S. Department of Agriculture) Unveils Historic Improvements to Meals Served in America's Schools: *New Standards Will Improve the Health and Well Being of 32 Million Kids Nationwide*, Release No. 0023.12 *Last Modified: 09/27/2013.* (http://www.usda.gov/wps/portal/usda/usdamediafb?contentid=2012/01/0023.xml&printable=true)

Text 2

1 First Lady Michelle Obama and Agriculture Secretary Tom Vilsack today unveiled new standards for school meals that will result in healthier meals for kids across the nation. The new meal requirements will raise standards for the first time in more than fifteen years and improve the health and nutrition of nearly 32 million kids that participate in school meal programs every school day. The healthier meal requirements are a key component of the Healthy, Hunger-Free Kids Act, which was championed by the First Lady as part of her Let's Move! campaign and signed into law by President Obama.

2 "As parents, we try to prepare decent meals, limit how much junk food our kids eat, and ensure they have a reasonably balanced diet," said First Lady Michelle Obama. "And when we're putting in all that effort the last thing we want is for our hard work to be undone each day in the school cafeteria. When we send our kids to school, we expect that they won't be eating the kind of fatty, salty, sugary foods that we try to keep them from eating at home. We want the food they get at school to be the same kind of food we would serve at our own kitchen tables."

3 "Improving the quality of the school meals is a critical step in building a healthy future for our kids," said Vilsack. "When it comes to our children, we must do everything possible to provide them the nutrition they need to be healthy, active and ready to face the future—today we take an important step towards that goal."

4 The final standards make the same kinds of practical changes that many parents are already encouraging at home, including:

- Ensuring students are offered both fruits and vegetables every day of the week;
- Substantially increasing offerings of whole grain-rich foods;
- Offering only fat-free or low-fat milk varieties;

- Limiting calories based on the age of children being served to ensure proper portion size; and
- Increasing the focus on reducing the amounts of saturated fat, trans fats and sodium.

5 The USDA built the new rule around recommendations from a panel of experts convened by the Institute of Medicine—a gold standard for evidence-based health analysis. The standards were also updated with key changes from the 2010 Dietary Guidelines for Americans—the Federal government's benchmark for nutrition—and aimed to foster the kind of healthy changes at school that many parents are already trying to encourage at home, such as making sure that kids are offered both fruits and vegetables each day, more whole grains, and portion sizes and calorie counts designed to maintain a healthy weight.

1. **Part A.** In paragraph 3, U.S. Agriculture Secretary Tom Vilsack said, "Improving the quality of the school meals is a critical step in building a healthy future for our kids." What does critical mean in this sentence?

○ a. Unnecessary

○ b. Tasty or delicious

○ c. Essential or much needed

○ d. Good

Part B. Which detail is the most substantial in justifying your answer to Part A?

○ a. *We must do everything possible to provide them the nutrition they need.*

○ b. *The final standards make the same kinds of practical changes that many parents are already encouraging at home.*

○ c. *The new meal requirements will raise standards for the first time in more than fifteen years.*

○ d. *As parents, we try to prepare decent meals, limit how much junk food our kids eat, and ensure they have a reasonably balanced diet.*

2. Use three key details to create a summary of the passage. Cross out 2; number the remaining 3 in order.

The new meal requirements will raise standards for the first time in more than fifteen years.	
Making sure that kids are offered both fruits and vegetables each day, more whole grains, and portion sizes and calorie counts designed to maintain a healthy weight.	
"Improving the quality of the school meals is a critical step in building a healthy future for our kids," said Vilsack.	
The final standards make the same kinds of practical changes that many parents are already encouraging at home.	
As parents, we try to prepare decent meals, limit how much junk food our kids eat, and ensure they have a reasonably balanced diet.	

3. Part A. How does this document support the idea that parents and government want the same things for their children?

- ○ a. The author uses number evidence.
- ○ b. The author shares stories or anecdotes about various families.
- ○ c. The author makes connections to what parents do at home.
- ○ d. The author creates images for the reader.

Part B. Which two paragraphs best supports your answer for Part A?

- ☐ a. 1
- ☐ b. 2
- ☐ c. 3
- ☐ d. 4
- ☐ e. 5

Answers are on page 151.

Text 3

Healthy, Hunger-Free Kids Act—2010
Before/After Elementary School Lunch Menu
Comparison of Current NSLP Elementary Meals vs. New Elementary Meal

MONDAY	TUESDAY	WEDNESDAY	THURSDAY	FRIDAY
Before Bean and cheese burrito (5.3 oz) with mozzarella cheese (1 oz) Applesauce (1/4 c) Orange Juice (4 oz) 2% Milk (8 oz)	**Before** Hot dog on a bun (3 oz) with ketchup (4 T) Canned Pears (1/4 c) Raw celery and carrots (1/8 c each) Ranch dressing (1.75 T) Low fat chocolate milk (8 oz)	**Before** Pizza sticks (3.8 oz) With marinara sauce (1.4 c) Banana Raisins (1 oz) Whole milk (8 oz)	**Before** Breaded beef patty (4 oz) Ketchup (2 T) Wheat roll (2 oz) Frozen fruit juice bar (2.4 oz) 2% Milk (8 oz)	**Before** Cheese pizza (4.8 oz) Canned pineapple (1/4 c) Tater tots (1/2 c) Ketchup (2 T) Low fat chocolate milk (8 oz)
After Submarine sandwich (1 oz turkey on whole wheat roll) (5 oz low fat cheese) Refried beans (1/2 c) Jicama (1/4 c) Green pepper strips (1/4 c) Low fat ranch dip (1 oz) Cantaloupe wedges (1/2 c) Skim milk (8 oz)	**After** Whole wheat spaghetti with meat sauce (1/2 c) Whole wheat roll Green beans cooked (1/2 c) Broccoli (1/2 c) Cauliflower (1/2 c) Low fat ranch dip (1 oz) Kiwi halves (1/2 c) Low fat 1% milk (8 oz)	**After** Chef salad w/low fat dressing (1.5 oz) Whole wheat soft pretzel (2.5 oz) Corn, cooked (1.2 c) Carrots, raw (1/4 c) Low fat ranch dip (1 oz) Banana Skim milk (8 oz)	**After** Oven-baked fish nuggets (2 oz) with whole wheat roll Mashed potatoes (1/2 c) Steamed broccoli (1/2 c) Peaches—canned in juice (1/2 c) Skim milk (8 oz) Tartar sauce (1.5 oz)	**After** Whole wheat cheese pizza (1 slice) Baked sweet potato fries (1/2 c) Grape tomatoes, raw (1/4 c) Low fat ranch dip (1 oz) Applesauce (1/2 c) Low fat 1% milk (8 oz)

http://www.fns.usda.gov/cnd/Governance/Legislation/cnr_chart.jpg

1. Use the following statements to complete the chart.

   a. low fat milk

   b. juice

   c. more fresh vegetables and fruits

   d. more whole grains

   e. more canned fruits

   f. low fat cheese

OLD MENU	BOTH	NEW MENU

2. **Part A.** What conclusion can be drawn after analyzing the new meal menu?

   ○ a. With the new, healthy changes, every meal will look similar, just be healthier.

   ○ b. With the new, healthy changes, most meals will look very different in order to make them healthier.

   ○ c. With the new, healthy changes, there will be very few changes in meals.

   ○ d. With the new, healthy changes, kids will avoid buying lunch.

   Part B. Which day(s) of the week best supports the statement in Part A? You may choose more than one answer.

   ☐ a. All of the days

   ☐ b. Tuesday

   ☐ c. Wednesday

   ☐ d. Friday

Answers are on page 153.

Once you have read or viewed three texts, you will be asked to construct a research-based essay. This means you MUST use proof from all three documents in your essay. Read the research task below:

> **Research Task**
>
> You have read two texts and examined a sample menu, all evaluating the claim that school cafeterias need to serve healthier meals. Write an essay that compares and contrasts the evidence each source uses to support this claim. Which document provides the strongest argument? Be sure to use evidence from all three sources to support your response.

First, let's examine the prompt and figure out what the task is asking you to do. Look at the prompt again. Which sentence or sentences is telling you the task, or what you need to do in this part of the test? Underline the task in the prompt above.

You should have underlined: Write an essay that compares and contrasts the evidence each source uses to support this claim. Which document provides the strongest argument?

I know I need to write an essay, so this gives me a structure for my writing. I'll need an introductory paragraph, body paragraphs to support ideas, and a conclusion paragraph. I also know that I must "compare and contrast" the evidence from each source. This means, I need to look for similarities and differences between the evidence in each text. Furthermore, I need to decide which document has the best argument and why. Last, I need to make sure I include evidence, or proof, from all three resources.

We know what our essay is about. Let's move on to the next step, gathering evidence. You cannot plan your essay until you have found your evidence. For this task, begin by highlighting evidence in each text that supports the claim, schools need healthier meals. You can simply underline in the article. Then, you need to look for similarities and differences within the evidence. Ask yourself, how did the author convince the reader that cafeteria food needs to be healthier?

To Do

1. Highlight evidence in each text that supports the claim.
2. Look for similarities and differences.
3. Decide which document has the best evidence.

Prewriting

How well you prewrite could very well make the difference between a passing and failing score on this part of the PARCC. This seems strange since the prewriting is not graded. Prewriting is important because the better you plan, the easier time you will have writing. Use five to ten minutes to plan and organize your writing. By using that time, you will actually need less time to write your essay. We will go through each step and give you opportunities to practice. The more you practice prewriting, the easier it will be when you take the test.

Below, you can see the evidence I would highlight for this question. You should underline your evidence in each article. Go back to the text now and search for sentences that prove healthier eating is necessary in school cafeterias.

School Lunches: Are They Healthy? (K. Perillo)	New School Meal Standards (USDA)	Sample Menu (USDA)
Close to 18 percent of children between the ages of 6 and 11 are obese and approximately one-third of children are either overweight or obese. (number) Many parents are unaware of the food being eaten by their children at school. They assume their son or daughter is eating a healthy, well-balanced meal. Samantha, a fifth grader, reported eating pizza and chips every day for lunch. (story)	"As parents, we try to prepare decent meals, limit how much junk food our kids eat, and ensure they have a reasonably balanced diet," said First Lady Michelle Obama. "And when we're putting in all that effort the last thing we want is for our hard work to be undone each day in the school cafeteria." (expert opinion) "Improving the quality of the school meals is a critical step in building a healthy future for our kids," said Vilsack. (expert opinion) aimed to foster the kind of healthy changes at school that many parents are already trying to encourage at home, such as making sure that kids are offered both fruits and vegetables each day, more whole grains, and portion sizes and calorie counts designed to maintain a healthy weight. (example)	(visual example) Before: Bean and cheese burrito Canned pears Raw celery and carrots with ranch dressing Low fat chocolate milk Breaded beef patty Cheese pizza After: Turkey and cheese submarine sandwich Kiwi halves Low fat 1% milk or skim Low fat ranch dip Baked fish Whole wheat cheese pizza

After you highlight your evidence, you can now plan the essay. This is done by prewriting. Prewriting is the place to organize your thoughts so you have an easier time writing the essay. The best way to organize your thoughts is by using a graphic organizer. A graphic organizer is a picture or chart that helps you split the essay into different parts to help you keep all of your thoughts in order. Since there are five parts to the persuasive essay—introduction, three body paragraphs, and the conclusion—we need a graphic organizer that has five parts. We like to create a drawing that is easy to draw and easy to split into five parts. Using the drawing, it makes it easier to remember the different parts of the essay, in case you forget. The drawing we are going to use in this book is a piece of cake because we think, if you follow and practice all of the advice in this book, the PARCC will be a piece of cake! Now let's look at our piece of cake and what each part represents.

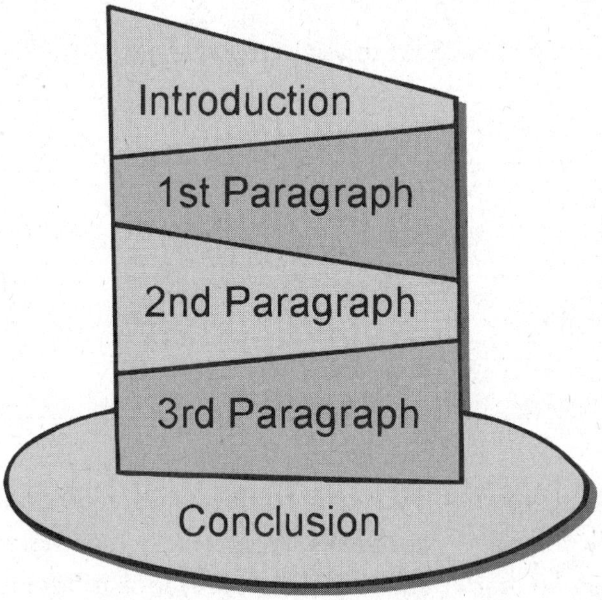

See? A piece of cake. How do we fill it in? We have to go step by step and fill in each part so we are ready to write our essay. Let's go back to our writing prompt and remember what our choice is. Here is the prompt again.

> **Research Task**
>
> Write an essay that compares and contrasts the evidence each source uses to support this claim. Which document provides the strongest argument?

The introduction is the frosting. It is tasty, people usually look forward to it, and you can get a good idea if the rest of the cake is going to be good. The introduction is very important and has three parts. They are the interest catcher, thesis statement, and three reasons. The interest catcher will be the first part of your essay, but the thesis statement is the most important, so we will start with that part first. Each is explained below.

Writing a Thesis Statement

The thesis statement is the one sentence that will tell the reader what your essay is about. If every other sentence is eliminated from the essay, the thesis statement will tell the reader what you think, feel, and believe. Ask yourself how the body will be organized. This will allow you to properly plan.

What will this essay be about? Write your thesis below:

Excellent work! Next, you need your supporting reasons or ideas. They should be clear and be directly related to your thesis. What will each paragraph be about? You just wrote your thesis, so read it again. This part may look different depending on if you are persuading or explaining. If you are persuading, you will have three reasons to convince people to agree with your idea. If you are explaining, you will need to think about the three ideas for your essay.

Let's take a look at two different examples.

Persuasive Thesis Example: Let's say you have been researching a destination for the fifth-grade class trip. You have read about Island Beach State Park, The Aquarium, and the Philadelphia Zoo. You decide to write about going to Island Beach State Park.

Your thesis may look like this: The field trip that our school should choose is Island Beach State Park.

Reason #1: Island Beach State Park has educational opportunities.

Reason #2: It will allow the students to experience valuable outdoor education.

Reason #3: Even though the trip is educational, students will also have fun.

Each reason will be explained and supported in a body paragraph. The reasons should be clear but do not need to be too specific. In this case, your essay is explaining how each text presents their evidence, and then presenting an argument as to which document has the strongest evidence. Your thesis may look a little different. Remember, the thesis tells the reader what the essay will be about. Here, the essay will compare and contrast how each text presents a claim and then decide which is the strongest.

Thesis Statement and Three Ideas: The research presented strong evidence to show schools need healthier cafeterias in order to promote healthy eating. The three documents have slight *similarities* in how they present evidence, but significant *differences.* Of the three documents, one stood out as having the *strongest argument.*

This essay, will contain one paragraph about similarities, one paragraph about differences, and one identifying the article with the strongest argument.

Interest Catcher

The first part of your essay should give the reader an idea about your essay, but not tell them everything. It should make them want to read more. It can be more than one sentence, but should not take you too long to write. There are a few different types of interest catchers you can use. They are the rhetorical question, startling fact, and descriptive scene. Let's look at each one. Then, you can practice creating an interest catcher for each one.

Rhetorical Question

A rhetorical question is a question that does not require an answer. They are meant to get someone's attention or encouraging them to think about a topic. An example of a rhetorical question could be, "Why does this always happen to me?" or "Can you believe they are closing the movie theater?" For our essay it could be, "Do you eat a healthy school lunch each day you leave the lunch line?" The person who is asking the question doesn't need you to answer. They just want you to think about the topic or what is happening.

Startling Fact

Nothing gets someone's attention faster than a shocking fact or idea. If it is something that they never thought about before, they will be interested in knowing more. You can use math and create a number that will get someone's attention. "Eighty-seven percent of fifth graders at our school have never been to the ocean." It should be something that will cause the reader to say, "I can't believe that." A startling fact could be "More students failed the test than passed." That would get your attention. You would worry that you were one of the people who failed.

Descriptive Scene

A descriptive scene is the most difficult of the three types of interest catcher. It means exactly what it says. You start the essay with a short description of a scene. If you do it right, the reader will have a picture in his or her head that will give you the opportunity to get your point across to him or her. A descriptive scene could be more than one sentence. Here is an example:

Imagine students exiting the cafeteria line and heading to the garbage can to quickly throw away the fruit and vegetables from their tray, quickly creating piles of wasted food. Imagine the fruit and vegetables being replaced with chips or cookies. Now, imagine students tired and unable to stay alert and ready to learn through the last period of the day.

Do you have a picture in your head of what the students are doing in the cafeteria? The reader has started an image of students wasting healthy food and the impacts of a poor diet. These are all things you can see, and it gives you the opportunity to convince the reader that eating a healthy lunch is an important idea. Are you ready to try some on your own? Great! Read the prompt one more time, and then create your own interest catchers.

Research Task

You have read two texts and examined a sample menu, all evaluating the claim that school cafeterias need to serve healthier meals. Write an essay that compares and contrasts the evidence each source uses to support this claim. Which document has the strongest argument? Be sure to use evidence from all three sources to support your response.

Practice

Write three different openings for your essay about healthy eating.

1. Rhetorical Question: ______________________________

____

2. Startling Fact: ______________________________

____

3. Descriptive Scene (don't write more than two or three sentences):

____

____

____

____

____

Excellent job. This may seem like a lot, especially since this part of the prewriting is only for the introduction, but if you work hard on these parts, writing the essay is going to be a piece of cake!

Body Paragraphs and Supporting Details

Right now, you might be asking yourself, "Why do I have to prewrite for the supporting paragraphs if I already have my three reasons or paragraph ideas?" This is where most students lose points on essays. The writer has three good reasons or ideas but does not write anything to support them. Because of this, the writer receives a lower score than expected. For the prewriting part of this essay, we are going to concentrate on how you can support your reasons. There are several strategies you can use to help you be more convincing. We are going to focus on using examples, statistics, expert opinion, and positive/negative consequences.

The three layers of cake are your supporting paragraphs. Of course, the number of layers can vary if you have more or less than three ideas or reasons to write about. These layers are the important parts, the substance of your essay. Without these paragraphs, the readers will not know why they should believe your side or opinion. To support your three reasons you need details, specific details. These strategies are a way for you to convince the reader to believe your opinion. Each technique will be explained, and then you will search for an example within the research articles.

Examples

Authors use examples all the time to support their writing. Often an example may be in the form of a story, or anecdote. When you read these, you relate and connect, or so the author hopes. Examples are a really easy way to show the reader what you mean, while anecdotes allow the reader to connect. Sometimes examples or anecdotes create a feeling for the reader that EVERYONE shares a certain belief. This is called bandwagon. Look back at the research and find an example or story to support healthy cafeteria eating.

Why is this convincing?

Statistics

Statistics is a fancy way of saying numbers. You use the numbers and percentages to prove your point when writing. Number evidence is great evidence. When you are reading for the research task, keep your eyes open for numbers. Anytime you see really good number evidence, highlight it. Look back at the research and find an example of statistical data, or number evidence.

Why is this convincing?

Expert Opinion

If you have trouble with a math problem, whom do you ask? Your math teacher, right? That is because your math teacher is the expert. If you have a bad cold, you would go to the doctor because he or she is the expert that helps you stay healthy. So in an essay, you would use an use an expert to help prove a point. In the articles you read, you will find several examples of expert opinion. Let's practice one more time.

Look back at the text for this research task. See if you can find a good example of expert opinion. Make sure you note the name of the article where you found the proof.

Why is this person an expert?

Positive and Negative Consequences

Positive consequences means that, when you do something, good things will happen. Negative consequences mean that the result of your actions will cause something bad. You can choose one or the other for your essay. We have an example below for both positive and negative consequences. Read the examples and then you will give it a try.

Idea: Even though the trip is educational, students will also have fun.

Positive consequence: If our class has the chance to go to Island Beach State Park, many students will learn about ways to keep the ocean clean and be friendlier to the environment.

Negative consequence: If our class does not go to Island Beach State Park, many students will not understand why it is important to have clean oceans.

Let's Practice

Now it is your turn. Choose positive or negative consequences and write a sentence supporting your reason.

Write a positive consequence below:

If lunch regulations are stricter, --

Write a negative consequence below:

Without lunch regulations, --

Conclusion

The conclusion is not part of the piece of cake. It is the plate, supporting all of the reasons and support you have written so far. Without a solid plate, the whole cake would fall down. The conclusion has three parts to it, and two of them are very easy to do. The three parts of the conclusion are restating the thesis, restating your main ideas, and ending with a clincher.

When you are restating your thesis and ideas, you want to write it in a different way. Since we are prewriting now, you do not need to worry about restating them in your graphic organizer, but you do need to make sure they are written in the conclusion of your essay. The part of the conclusion that you do need to think about when you are prewriting is your final statement. This is called your clincher. You may choose to ask another rhetorical question or end with a thought provoking statement. The best option is to revisit your interest catcher. If you asked rhetorical questions in the beginning, try to answer them at the end. If you started with a descriptive scene, revise the scene for your closing.

Here is what the prewriting for the example essay might look like:

Thesis Statement: The research presented strong evidence to show schools need healthier cafeterias in order to promote healthy eating.

#1—similarities

#2—differences

#3—USDA most convincing

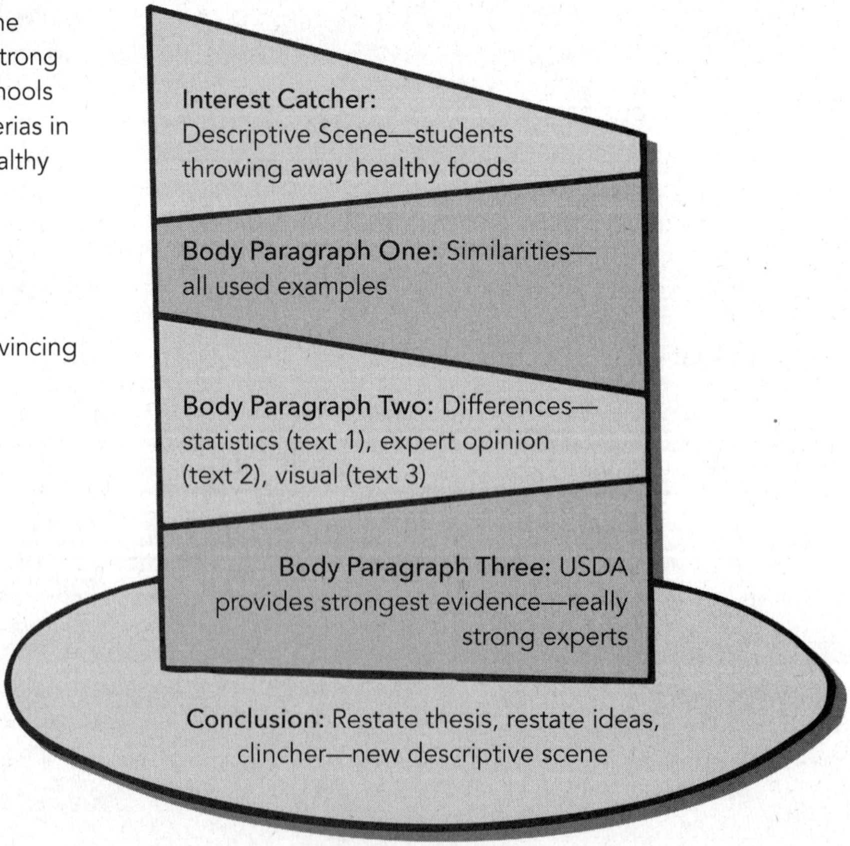

What do you notice about this graphic organizer? Did you notice that everything is not written out completely? This is because the prewriting is the time for you to think about the essay and write down ideas about what the essay will include. You will add the details when you write the essay.

Here is an example of the completed research task essay.

Imagine students exiting the cafeteria line and heading to the garbage can to quickly throw away the fruit and vegetables from their tray. Piles of wasted food build higher and higher throughout the day. Imagine the fruit and vegetables being replaced with chips or cookies. Now, imagine students tired and unable to stay alert and ready to learn through the last period of the day. Many people believe kids need to eat healthier. The research presented strong evidence to show schools need healthier cafeterias in order to promote healthy eating. The three documents have slight similarities in how they presented evidence, but significant differences. Of the three documents, one stood out as having the strongest argument.

The main way all three texts are alike is that they each provide valid examples to support healthier meals. For example, the article by K. Perillo states, "Samantha, a fifth grader, reported eating pizza and chips every day for lunch." This is a specific example that allows the reader to connect. Parents are wondering if their child is doing the same thing as Samantha everyday. Kids are nodding in agreement. Furthermore, the USDA explains in their release that the new standards "aimed to foster the kind of healthy changes at school that many parents are already trying to encourage at home, such as making sure that kids are offered both fruits and vegetables each day, more whole grains, and portion sizes and calorie counts designed to maintain a healthy weight." The author specifically gives an example of the healthy choices and even says, "such as." Again, this clearly shows the author's message that parents agree with the guidelines. Last, the sample menu is comprised of examples of meal options both with the old and new standards or guidelines. This is meant to show how similar menu items, can be slightly altered to have a much healthier meal. All of these examples clearly show how important it is for kids to eat healthier.

In contrast, there are numerous differences in how each article supports this claim. For instance, the second text released by the USDA focuses on expert opinion to convince readers that school lunch rules need to change. The document quotes Michele Obama saying, "As parents, we try to prepare decent meals, limit how much junk food our kids eat, and ensure they have a reasonably balanced diet. And when we're putting in all that effort the last thing we want is for our hard work to be undone each day in the school cafeteria." As the First Lady, Michele Obama's words are powerful and convincing. Other parents can relate to what she says and agree that healthy eating needs to continue in the schools. Additionally, the first article by K. Perillo offers statistic evidence. When she says, "Over 9 million...." The sample lunch menu relies on visually showing people the comparison between school meals under the old regulations versus the new regulations. After examining the menu, easy changes such as going to whole wheat crust on the pizza can make a healthy impact on kids. All of these examples prove there are many different ways to support the same claim.

Text 1 is the most convincing because it offers the most varied evidence. For example, the author uses number evidence, story evidence, and expert opinion. Perillo states, "According to the Center for Disease Control, close to 18 percent of children between the ages of 6 and 11 are obese and approximately one-third of children are either overweight or obese." This is a startling number that shows the need to help kids eat healthier. Otherwise, these kids will grow up to be unhealthy adults, and they may end up with heart disease or high blood pressure. Furthermore, the author uses stories about real kids like fifth-grader Samantha. When asked about the complete lunch, she said, "No one eats that! I don't know why they even offer it." This is important because it shows how much food is being wasted right now. The rules are necessary, but kids need to actually eat the food to make it matter. The author is searching for a way to encourage kids to eat more healthy foods.

In conclusion, parents, schools, and kids need to all work together to reevaluate the current regulations and find a way to make cafeteria food healthier. Providing a better menu with more fruits and vegetables is a good first step, but now we need to find a way to decrease the amount of food wasted and increase the amount of fruits and vegetables eaten. Imagine students exiting the cafeteria line with piles of fresh fruits and vegetables. Now, imagine every student eating those healthy foods. Better yet, imagine students having the necessary energy to do their best work, even at the end of the school day.

Hints for Success

If you follow all of the parts of essay writing included in this chapter, you should have an easier time on this part of the PARCC.

- Remember to prewrite.
- Include a thesis statement.
- Start with an interest catcher.
- Support your ideas with evidence from the text.
- End with a clincher.

There are, however, a few more things that you can do to push your score to the highest level possible. Use the extra practice below to boost your writing to the next level.

Transitions

Transitions are the bridges between paragraphs and sentences in your essay. They are the words that signal the reader that you are moving on to a new idea or helping to explain an old idea. Different transitions will work better in different situations. Some transitions will show you are starting a new idea, whereas others signal an explanation or conclusion. Use the chart below to help you when you write.

Transitions for a first evidence:	Transitions for additional evidence:	Transitions for explaining evidence:
For instance In fact As evidence For example	Furthermore Additionally Most important	Therefore As a result This means

Transitions for showing the opposite:	Transitions for showing a similar idea:	Transitions for concluding a paragraph or essay:
However In contrast On the other hand	Likewise Similarly	In conclusion Thus In summary In brief Finally

Let's Practice

It's time for a quick practice. After you finish, check your answers in the back of the book.

1. Which of the following transitions would be appropriate to use when starting the paragraph <u>after</u> the introduction? Check all that apply.

   ☐ a. Furthermore

   ☐ b. However

   ☐ c. In fact

   ☐ d. Therefore

   ☐ e. For instance

2. Which of the following transitions would be appropriate to use when starting a paragraph that adds evidence to the essay? Check all that apply.

☐ a. Furthermore

☐ b. However

☐ c. Additionally

☐ d. Therefore

☐ e. In conclusion

3. Which transitions would be used to start a sentence explaining evidence? Check all that apply.

☐ a. For example

☐ b. First of all

☐ c. In conclusion

☐ d. Next

☐ e. Therefore

Answers are on page 153.

Word Choice

Using strong words helps your writing be clear and more enjoyable for the reader. A great writer can pick the perfect word at the right place. Remember to use the best vocabulary you can when writing your essay. Do not write "good" when you can write "fantastic." Avoid "bad" when you can use "horrible." The reader will have a better understanding of your essay, and your sophisticated vocabulary will help increase your score. Be careful. It is OK if you misspell a word here or there, but make sure if you use difficult vocabulary that you know how to spell the word. If you mean to write "horrible" but spell it "horible," that is not too bad. If you spell it "haribel," however, the reader may not understand what word you mean. The PARCC is a chance for you to show how much you know, so be awesome, stupendous, and excellent, not just good.

Sentence Structure

In the last chapter of this book, there are lessons and examples about grammar. Make sure you do all of the work in that chapter so you do not make simple mistakes. One part of that chapter that is worth repeating is sentence structure. Writing complete sentences helps the reader understand what you are writing about. If the reader has to stop and reread sentences because they do not make sense, are incomplete, or are too long, they may give your essay a lower score. Make sure every sentence is complete and makes sense.

A complete sentence has a subject and a predicate. The subject tells the reader who or what the sentence is about and the predicate tells the action of the subject. To be complete, a sentence MUST have both a subject and predicate. For example, *The quiet boy* is not a complete sentence. It has a subject, but we don't know what the quiet boy is doing. *The quiet boy was too shy to go to the school dance.* Now there is a subject and a predicate.

A run-on sentence is more than one complete sentence connected without a conjunction or punctuation. This is also incorrect when writing. *The quiet boy was too shy to go to the school dance instead he stayed home and watched a movie with his family.* This is two independent sentences combined into one. *The quiet boy was too shy to go to the school dance* is one sentence and *instead he stayed home and watched a movie with his family* is it's own sentence. The author either needs to separate into two sentences or combine with a conjunction. *The quiet boy was too shy to go to the school dance, so instead he stayed home and watched a movie with his family.* You need a comma before the "so" because these are two independent sentences.

Let's Practice

Are you ready for a quiz? Fill in the blanks or circle the correct answer on each multiple-choice question. Check your answers when you are done.

1. A complete sentence has a s .... and p ....

2. Which of the following sentences are complete sentences? Check all that apply.

   ☐ a. I quickly ran to the store down the street from my house.
   ☐ b. Ran quickly down the street.
   ☐ c. I walked.
   ☐ d. After running to the store.

3. Which sentences below are well-constructed, complete sentences? Check all that apply.

   ☐ a. I took a test.
   ☐ b. I ran a mile it took a long time.
   ☐ c. I fell off my chair when he told me a joke.
   ☐ d. Laughing so hard.
   ☐ e. After I finish studying.

Answers are on page 153.

Practice Time!

It is time to practice the research task from beginning to end. Read each passage and complete the questions. Remember to use all your strategies from Chapter 1. Then carefully read the prompt, underline the important parts, figure out what the prompt is asking you to write, highlight evidence, prewrite, and construct your essay. A blank piece of cake prewriting template has been given to you, but none of the information has been filled in. On the test, you can easily draw a rectangle and divide it into five parts to represent your piece of cake. An example essay and explanation can be found at the end of the chapter. Good Luck.

HINTS FOR SUCCESS

- Read the prompt carefully and identify your task words. There may be more than one thing you need to address.
- Highlight your evidence in the text. In this part of the test, you MUST use evidence from each article.
- Plan your essay. Remember, every essay has an introduction with a thesis statement, a body with supporting evidence and explanation, and a conclusion to wrap it all up.
- Your essay should be at least four paragraphs long.
- Use sophisticated transitions.
- Be detailed.

Directions: In this part of the test, you will read three articles. Answer the questions that appear after each passage.

Text 1

An excerpt from *Tim Tebow: A Promise Kept*

by Mike Klis (2012)

Critics, Many Silenced

1 To recognize that Tim Tebow is, perhaps, the most popular athlete in America tells only half the story. The other half is that Tebow is probably also the most criticized player. More accurately, Tebow is regarded by many as football's most polarizing player. This means most fans either really like or really dislike him. There's no in-between.

2 His popularity is easy to understand. The criticism is often baffling. Tebow never says a bad word about anybody. It's obvious that whether he's playing well or not-so-well that he gives it his all.

3 Most of all, Tebow is a winner. No matter how poorly a game is going, he never quits and often figures out how to win at the end. Yet, NFL analysts like Jimmy Johnson, Shannon Sharpe, Trent Dilfer, and Joe Theismann, among others, questioned whether Tebow was consistent enough to succeed because of major flaws in his passing motion.

4 When it came to Tebow, even active players broke the unwritten code that you don't criticize other players, including opponents. Baltimore linebacker Terrell Suggs joined active players Steve Smith, Jermichael Finley, and Joe Flacco in ripping Tebow. But no one was more mean-spirited than Merrill Hoge, former NFL running back and current ESPN analyst. In August 2011, while the Broncos were still in training camp and had yet to play their first pre-season game, Hoge tweeted: "It's embarrassing to think the Broncos could win with Tebow!"

5 A few months later, after Tebow had directed the Broncos to their first playoff appearance in six years, it was Hoge who blushed.

6 After Tebow's remarkable 20-yard touchdown run with 58 seconds left beat the New York Jets, 17–13 on Nov. 17, the lefty who critics said couldn't play quarterback had led the Broncos to three wins in a row. He was 4–1 as a starter for a team that was 1–4 before he took control.

> In the stretch between November 1, 2009, and October 23, 2011, the day Tebow started his first game for the Broncos, Denver's 7–24 record was the worst in the NFL. The Broncos lost 8 of their final 10 games in 2009, were 4–12 in 2010, and then 1–4 to start the 2011 season. Tebow then won 7 of his first eight starts of 2011, meaning he generated as many wins in eight games as the Broncos had in their previous 31 games when their quarterback was primarily Kyle Orton.

1. Part A. In paragraph 1, Mike Klis refers to Tebow as football's most polarizing player. In this sentence, what is the definition of polarizing?

- ○ a. Resulting in admiration from people
- ○ b. Causing people to dislike him
- ○ c. Causing people to gravitate towards him
- ○ d. Causing people to separate into two opposite groups

Part B. Underline the sentence in paragraph 1 that best supports this definition.

To recognize that Tim Tebow is, perhaps, the most popular athlete in America tells only half the story. The other half is that Tebow is probably also the most criticized player. More accurately, Tebow is regarded by many as football's most polarizing player. This means most fans either really like or really dislike him. There's no in-between.

2. Part A. What is a main idea from the excerpt?

- ○ a. Tebow is one of the best football players ever.
- ○ b. It is difficult to understand why people do not like Tebow.
- ○ c. More people dislike Tebow, than like him.
- ○ d. Tebow brought the Broncos to their first playoff series in six years.

Part B. Which two details best support your main idea?

- ☐ a. "It's embarrassing to think the Broncos could win with Tebow!"
- ☐ b. His popularity is easy to understand.
- ☐ c. Tebow never says a bad word about anybody.
- ☐ d. He was 4–1 as a starter for a team that was 1–4 before he took control.
- ☐ e. No matter how poorly a game is going, he never quits and often figures out how to win at the end.

3. Part A. How does the author feel about Tim Tebow?

- ○ a. He believes Tim Tebow is inconsistent.
- ○ b. He thinks Tim Tebow does not have enough football experience.
- ○ c. He does not like Tim Tebow.
- ○ d. He respects Tim Tebow.

Part B. In the paragraph below, underline the evidence that best supports your answer to Part A:

Most of all, Tebow is a winner. No matter how poorly a game is going, he never quits and often figures out how to win at the end. Yet, NFL analysts like Jimmy Johnson, Shannon Sharpe, Trent Dilfer, and Joe Theismann, among others, questioned whether Tebow was consistent enough to succeed because of major flaws in his passing motion. When it came to Tebow, even active players broke the unwritten code that you don't criticize other players, including opponents. Baltimore linebacker Terrell Suggs joined active players Steve Smith, Jermichael Finley, and Joe Flacco in ripping Tebow.

Answers are on page 153.

Text 2

An excerpt from *The One Direction Story: An Unauthorized Biography* by Danny White

Read the following text and answer the questions.

WHAT MAKES THEM BEAUTIFUL

The band [One Direction] also performed their single on the Cowell-created game show *Red or Black*. This appearance turned out to be a less happy experience. For part of the song the audience were shown a specially acted video of the band traveling to the television studio via the subway underground, singing the first two verses and choruses on the train among the fans, and then being chased from the underground station, down the road to the TV studio by screaming fans. What was meant as a simple fun gimmick was instead interpreted by some viewers as evidence that the band were being shielded from giving a full performance due to a lack of talent when it came to live performances.

One would have thought that seeing Harry clearly sing the a capella section live onstage should have been enough to dispel those thoughts. His nerves—and breathlessness having danced around on-stage—were both clear. His hands shook as he sang and his eyes looked more than a little anxious. When he completed the solo part successfully, he breathed a sigh of relief, Niall patted him on the shoulder, and the band launched back into the full crashing chorus. It had all been all right—or had it?

When they came off air, Harry said he "felt a little sorry for himself" over the way he had let his nerves show. He logged onto Twitter and searched to see what was being said about him online. He was devastated by the extent of the abuse that he found.

Louis tried to comfort him but realized there was not much he could do. "I felt powerless," said Louis later. The band rallied round Harry and assured him that they and the fans still adored him. For many fans, Harry's nerves had only made him seem more real and adorable. It reminded the fans that this was a new band comprised of young men. One Direction were on the way to becoming the top dogs of British pop but they retained the image of the underdog. They were being styled and managed well. Since they left The X Factor, they had been physically transformed only to an extent—they looked and behaved more like pop stars but were still recognizable as the boys who had appeared for their first auditions.

1. **Part A.** In the last paragraph, what is the definition of rallied? The band rallied around Harry.

   ○ a. To show kindness
   ○ b. Come together to sing
   ○ c. Come together for a common purpose
   ○ d. To become famous

   Part B. Which detail provides the best support for Part A?

   ○ a. *assured him that they and the fans still adored him*
   ○ b. *he "felt a little sorry for himself" over the way he had let his nerves show.*
   ○ c. *Louis tried to comfort him but realized there was not much he could do.*
   ○ d. *Harry's nerves had only made him seem more real and adorable.*

2. **Part A.** In paragraph 4, the author states, "One Direction were on the way to becoming the top dogs of British pop but they retained the image of the underdog." What does this mean?

   ○ a. The boys were still young and nervous.
   ○ b. The boys did not have a good image, and people disliked them.
   ○ c. The boys were popular, but people were rooting for them like they weren't so popular.
   ○ d. The boys were popular, and everyone knew it.

Part B. Which detail provides the best support for Part A?

- ○ a. *Louis tried to comfort him but realized there was not much he could do. "I felt powerless," said Louis later.*
- ○ b. *Harry's nerves had only made him seem more real and adorable.*
- ○ c. *He was devastated by the extent of the abuse that he found.*
- ○ d. *They looked and behaved more like pop stars but were still recognizable as the boys who had appeared for their first auditions.*

3. Place each main idea statement into the chart below:

1. Being kind and staying positive are more powerful than negativity.
2. Always do your best, regardless of what people say.
3. Friends help get you through tough times.
4. Everyone gets nervous.
5. It takes courage to overcome put downs from others.
6. At times, everyone needs to rely on personal strength to overcome the tough times.

TIM TEBOW	BOTH	HARRY FROM ONE DIRECTION

Answers are on page 154.

Text 3

Excerpt from *Justin Bieber Confidential* by Robert Scott (2014)

Read the following text and answer the questions.

1 Justin made an effort to find the time to meet and greet his fans and sign autographs and pose for photographs. His team often posted videos of such events on his YouTube channel, and the singer graciously left messages there. In one he said, "Hey guys, it's Justin. I just wanted to add a note thanking you personally for all the support. You are helping a kid from a small town chase a dream, and I am forever grateful. Thanks to you, my family is having a chance at a better life, and I am getting to go and see places I could have never dreamed of."

2 He added, "This is just the beginning, but I wanted to let you know how thankful I am because without you this would never have happened." Such considerate moments on his internet presence served to endear Justin to his fans even more. Even some backstage jams while on tour would be filmed and placed online, giving his supporters a look at his working life behind the scenes. On August 4, 2011, he was filmed playing Kanye West's song "Heartless" and Drake's "Successful" on his guitar, and singing them with passion.

3 He also told MTV News, candidly discussing the album, "There's a lot of stuff that's not just about love. There are songs that teens can relate to, as far as parents not being together and divorce and just stuff that happens in everyday life. There are a lot of kids my age and their real life isn't "perfect," everything isn't perfect, so my album kind of <u>portrays</u> that. You just have to make the best of what you have. I'm looking forward to influencing others in a positive way."

4 "My message is: you can do anything if you put your mind to it. I grew up below the poverty line; I didn't have as much as other people did."

1. **Part A.** In paragraph 3, Justin states real life isn't perfect and his "album kind of portrays that." What does portrays mean in this sentence?

- O a. Perfect
- O b. Depicts or shows
- O c. Musical achievement
- O d. To act on stage

Part B. Choose the detail that best supports your answer to Part A.

- O a. *There are songs that teens can relate to, as far as parents not being together and divorce and just stuff that happens in everyday life.*
- O b. *You just have to make the best of what you have.*
- O c. *My family is having a chance at a better life.*
- O d. *You can do anything if you put your mind to it.*

2. **Part A.** How do paragraphs 1 and 2 contribute to Justin's views on fans?

- O a. Justin realizes he needs to tolerate his fans.
- O b. Justin allows fans to see him behind the scenes.
- O c. Justin is grateful to his fans because they are critical to his success.
- O d. Justin appreciates all the money spent by his fans.

Part B. Which detail best supports this claim?

- O a. *Thanks to you, my family is having a chance at a better life.*
- O b. *His team often posted videos of such events on his YouTube channel.*
- O c. *Considerate moments on his internet presence served to endear Justin to his fans even more.*
- O d. *He was filmed playing Kanye West's song "Heartless" and Drake's "Successful" on his guitar.*

Answers are on page 155.

Research Task

You read three short articles about young celebrities, Tim Tebow, Harry from One Direction, and Justin Bieber. Based on the text, what common lesson(s) have they learned since becoming famous? Write an essay using evidence from the text as support.

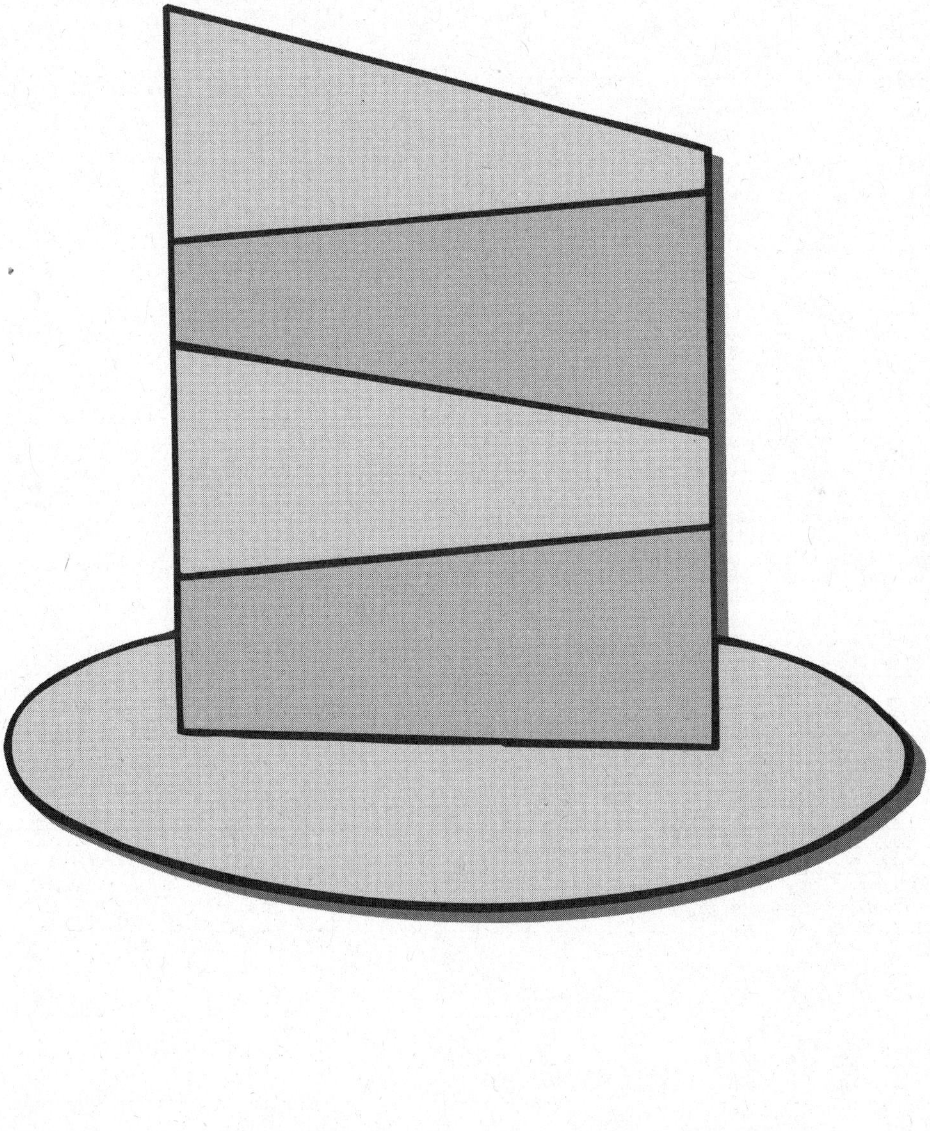

Use this checklist to assess your essay.

- [ ] I planned my essay before I started writing.
- [ ] My essay is at least four paragraphs long.
- [ ] I have an introduction paragraph.
- [ ] I have an interest catcher.
- [ ] I have a thesis statement.
- [ ] My body paragraphs use evidence from each text.
- [ ] I explained each evidence in detail.
- [ ] I used appropriate transition words.
- [ ] I have a conclusion that wraps up my thoughts and restates my thesis statement.
- [ ] I have a clincher.

Answers are on page 155.

References

Klis, Mike (2012). *Tim Tebow: A Promise Kept*. Hauppauge, NY: Barron's Educational Series.

Scott, Robert (2014). *Justin Bieber Confidential*. Hauppauge, NY: Barron's Educational Series.

White, Danny (2012). *The One Direction Story*. Hauppauge, NY: Barron's Educational Series.

Reading and Analyzing Literature

CHAPTER 3

Use the checklist to keep track of your work in this chapter.

- [ ] What Is Literature?
- [ ] Reading for Understanding
- [ ] Interacting with Text
- [ ] Using Context Clues
- [ ] Let's Practice
- [ ] Understanding Story Elements
- [ ] Figurative Language Review
- [ ] Answering Multiple-Choice Questions
- [ ] Prose Constructed Response (PCR)
- [ ] Practice Time!

What Is Literature?

One type of reading you will face on the PARCC is literature. There is no need to worry, because you already know all about this type of text. Literature simply means a story, so on this part of the test you will read a short story or passage from a story, answer questions, and construct an essay analyzing the text. When you analyze the text, you need to really think about the author's words, message, or theme.

Reading for Understanding

As you read literature, it is really important that you are using strategies to help you understand and remember the text. You will have a limited time to finish this part of the test, and you don't want to waste time rereading. Your goal is to **read and understand the first time**! Again, this happens when you take your time and use your reading strategies. Now, just like you heard in the informational text chapter, you might be tempted to look ahead and read the questions first, but you should not do this! You might be asking, "Why not?" Perhaps you've even had someone tell you this is a good strategy to use. If you read the questions ahead of time, you probably will not focus on all of the details of the story, and guess what? You will need ALL of the details of the story to analyze the text accurately. The only question you SHOULD read is the essay question. This allows you to search for proof as you read. On the PARCC, you can highlight. So when you practice, underline or highlight in the book.

Now, how can you accomplish this goal? Just like informational text, you are going to apply reading strategies and interact with the text. Remember, each time you use a strategy, you are telling your brain, "This is important information!" This may slow your reading down slightly, but it will be well worth it, if you don't have to go back later and reread for every question on the test. Take a few minutes to review the reading strategies below.

READING STRATEGIES

- **Predict:** Guess what will happen in the text.
- **Question:** Ask questions of the author and text.
- **Connect:** Make connections between the story, world events, or other text you have read, heard, or seen.
- **Visualize:** Picture what is happening in your head.
- **Summarize:** Stop periodically and retell what has happened so far in the story.
- **Infer:** Look for the clues, think about what you already know and make a guess or draw a conclusion.
- **Use Context Clues:** If you don't know a word, use the words around it to try and figure it out. Check if the author provided an example, synonym, or antonym to help you figure out the definition.

Let's give it a try. We're going to read two paragraphs from a story and practice interacting with the text. You will see my thoughts in parentheses. Afterward, you will have a chance to practice! We will need to slow down our reading in order to do this, but we will have an easier time remembering the story later!

"The Look"

As I sauntered through the front door, I saw my mom standing in the foyer, her arms crossed, and the look I knew all too well on her face. (I think this mom is angry. I wonder what happened?) It was the look that most mom's mastered early on in your childhood, the look that lets you know to knock it off or else. (I remember getting the look from my mom when I was arguing with my sister at a restaurant.) The worst-case scenario was walking through the front door and seeing that look waiting for you. I knew immediately I was in for it.

"Uh, hi Mom. How are you?" I asked forcing my big brown eyes to become even bigger and using my most innocent voice. (Why is the narrator using an innocent voice? Sounds like he did something wrong.) Mom didn't answer. Instead, she just stared at me, shaking her head. She was a lioness ready to pounce, and I just needed to figure out which antic she found out about. (What is an antic? It must be the reason the narrator was in trouble.) I was pretty sure she couldn't have found out about my trip to the mall but maybe it was what happened in math class. (I wonder what happened at the mall? Was the narrator cheating in math? Sounds like he gets in trouble a lot.)

What was going through your head as you read? Did you make a connection? Most of us have had an experience where we've been in big trouble with a parent. Did you have different questions pop into your head?

Interacting with Text

Read the next part of the story and try to interact with the text. To practice, write your predictions, questions, connections, and comments in the margin. Remember to slow down and really think about what you are reading.

"Would you like to explain this, Connor?" Mom said as she waved an envelope between the two of us. "I don't understand why you keep getting into all this trouble." She continued to shout as the paper jabbed back and forth. She looked like a knight trying to slay the evil dragon.

I could tell from the envelope it had been mailed from Wilson Elementary School. I had erased the message on the machine from my math teacher and the one from the principal, too. I guess they finally mailed a letter home explaining why I had in-school suspension last week. I had to think fast. Maybe I could still get out of this.

"I can explain, Mom," I quickly said. What now? How could I justify shooting spitballs at Jessica Johnson?

Although you have practiced writing down your thoughts, you will want to do these things in your head during the test. Writing them down will take too much time, but you should be thinking them. Remember, your goal is to read and understand the text the *first* time. By using reading strategies, you will remember and understand more of the story. As a result, the questions will be much easier to answer. Read the passage below and practice your strategies in your head. If there is something that really stands out, feel free to underline or write on the text.

Then I blurted out, "I didn't do it!" As soon as the words flew out of my mouth I wanted to take them back. I knew I shouldn't have said it, but I couldn't help myself. Now I was really in for it. "It was RJ! He sits next to me, and the teacher made a mistake. I didn't want to rat him out." I didn't know what was wrong with me. The lies were lava flowing from an active volcano. There was no stopping them.

"I'll take care of this immediately," my mom said with a sympathetic look on her face. Before I could protest, she picked up the phone and started to dial. I slunk into the chair, mortified, but not knowing what to say. I knew RJ's mom wouldn't believe him and he would be grounded for a month. I listened to my mom retell the story. Then she said the dreaded words. "I'm just disappointed that RJ let Connor get in trouble for something he did." I couldn't take it any longer.

"Stop Mom! I did it! I was sitting behind Jessica and I was angry that she had gotten an A on the test. I thought it would be funny to shoot spitballs into her hair. She would leave the room with all the tiny pieces of paper stuck in her head and people would laugh. It was wrong! I know it was wrong!"

At that moment, my mom hung up the phone without saying another word. She had a knowing smile on her face and she said in a very calm voice, "Go to your room." It was at that moment that I realized my mom was smarter than I thought. She knew all along I was lying. She had never dialed RJ's mom and I had admitted everything. All I could do was accept the consequence. I knew I deserved whatever punishment she gave me and I was sure it would be a big one.

Using Context Clues

As you read, you may get stuck on an unfamiliar word. Don't panic! Try to use context clues to figure it out. Let's go back to "The Look." Reread the first sentence.

> As I sauntered through the front door, I saw my mom standing in the foyer, her arms crossed, and the look I knew all too well on her face.

"Foyer" may be an unfamiliar word to you, but if you use the clues around it, you will probably be able to figure out its definition. Mom was standing in the foyer, so it sounds like a place, and the narrator saw Mom in the foyer as he walked through the front door. With these clues, the reader can make a guess that the foyer is the area of the house by the front door.

Let's Practice

Now, it's your turn to practice using context clues. Read the sentence from the passage and try to figure out the definition of each underlined word. Then, explain using evidence, or proof, from the text. Show how you figured out the definition. Check your answers in the back of the book when you are done.

1. Mom didn't answer. Instead, she just stared at me, shaking her head. She was a lioness ready to <u>pounce</u>, and I just needed to figure out which antic she found out about.

   Clues: --

   Definition: --

   ----

2. She continued to shout as the paper <u>jabbed</u> back and forth. She looked like a knight trying to slay the evil dragon.

   Clues: --

   Definition: --

Answers are on page 156.

Understanding Story Elements

In order to answer the questions on this part of the PARCC, you will need to understand the elements of a story. Sometimes the test may use a different word than you, and it is just a matter of knowing test vocabulary. Let's take some time to examine each element.

The Setting

The setting determines when and where the story takes place. Sometimes the author describes the setting within the story and sometimes you need to use the clues given to figure it out. This is an important element to the story because it can influence the tone or mood of the story. For example, if the author describes a dark, creaky, old house, with boarded up windows as the setting it may create a scary tone and make the reader feel a little nervous.

Where does "The Look" take place?

Do we know when it takes place?

How do you know this information? What clues from the story led to this conclusion?

You probably said the story takes place at Connor's house, and you would be correct. The author never tells us exactly when the story takes place but we can figure it out. Does it sound like the story is taking place a long time ago or far off in the future? There are telephones and the characters talk like someone would talk today. As readers, we can determine that the story is realistic fiction and probably takes place in recent times.

The Characters

Who is this story about? This is your main character. Usually there is a protagonist, or hero, in the story and an antagonist, opponent or villain, in the story. Other people in the story may be minor characters. The reader learns about each character through the character's actions, words, and thoughts. Again, the author may come right out and tell you about the character but more often, you need to figure it out from clues in the story. For example, if the author describes Connor slowly walking up to the old, creaky house with sweaty palms and a pale face, the reader can determine that Connor is scared. Let's think back to "The Look" one more time. Keep Connor's words, actions, and thoughts in mind as well as anything else the author revealed. List as many of Connor's character traits, as possible:

You may have listed some things the author told the reader such as Connor has big brown eyes and is in elementary school. Hopefully you used some clues from the text to dig deeper into Connor's personality. You may have said he was mean because he was shooting spitballs at Jessica or that he was sneaky because he wasn't being honest with his mom.

As you read a story, you want to keep a few questions in mind to help you learn about character:

- What physical traits do I know about the character?
- What do the character's thoughts, words, and actions tell me?
- How has the character changed throughout the story?

These questions may give you insight to other parts of the story.

The Plot

The plot is the sequence of events in the story. It focuses on the conflict, or problem, and how the character will resolve this problem. The plot usually follows a set structure, which you may have seen.

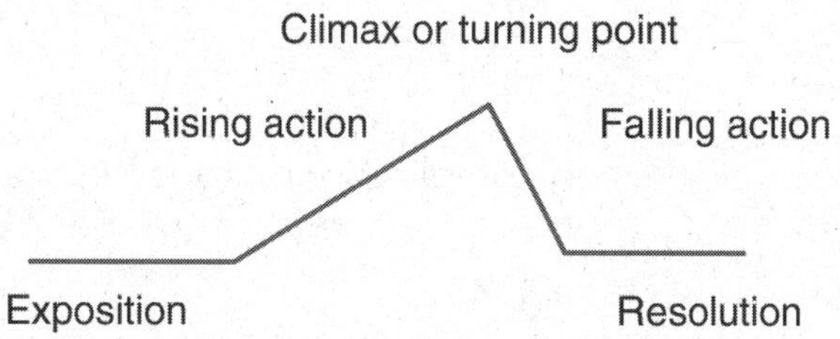

The plot begins with exposition, where the reader learns background information about the characters. It then moves to rising action. This is the biggest part of the story, where the most action takes place. There are several events, each building with excitement and anticipation. This is the part of the story where the character encounters problems or complications. Each conflict, or problem, gives the reader insight to the character. The character will probably attempt to solve the problem but fail for some reason. The rising action leads to the point of the story where the character tries to resolve the problem. He or she makes a decision that will change the course of the story. This is the climax or turning point of the story. The events that happen after the climax are the falling action. These events lead to the resolution. The resolution indicates how things will end for the character.

When analyzing the plot, ask yourself these questions:

- What is the conflict or problem of the story?
- What complications does the character face along the way?
- What is the turning point? (The point of the story where the character's decision will lead towards some type of solution)
- How is the conflict resolved?

Let's take a look at the plot to "The Look."

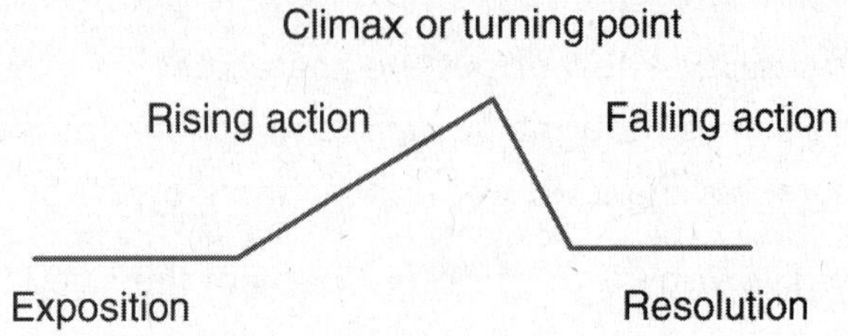

1. Exposition: What background information do we know?

---

2. Rising Action: What events and complications happen in the story?

---

3. Climax/Turning Point: In what part of the story does Connor make a decision that will change the course of the story?

4. Falling Action. What happens after the climax that will lead to the resolution?

---

5. Resolution: What will happen at the end of the story?

Answers are on page 157.

The Theme

Think of the theme as a life lesson. It is the moral or lesson the author would like the reader to learn. When trying to figure out the theme, you need to ask yourself the following questions:

- What does the author want the reader to learn from this story?
- How has the main character changed? What has he or she learned since the start of the story?

To find the theme of "The Look" ask yourself the following:

- What did Connor learn from this situation?
- What does the author want the reader to learn?

Write your answer on the lines below. Then, check your answers in the back of the book.

Answers are on page 157.

Figurative Language Review

When writing fiction, authors frequently use figurative language. This means that the author goes beyond the actual meaning of the word, phrase, or sentence in order to create an image or express an idea in a creative way. Let's review two common examples of figurative language. Not only will this help you better understand reading, but it will also prepare you for multiple-choice or open-ended questions.

1. A SIMILE compares two unlike objects using "like" or "as."

   The math problem was as difficult as completing brain surgery in the dark.

   The simile is comparing the math problem to brain surgery in the dark. The reader can infer it would be extremely difficult, if not impossible, to complete brain surgery in the dark. Therefore, the math problem must also be extremely difficult.

2. A METAPHOR makes a comparison of two unlike objects without using "like" or "as." Instead the author implies that something is something else and leaves the reader to make an inference or draw a conclusion.

   As the dog snarled, the pointy knives lining his fierce mouth scared me.

   This metaphor is comparing the dog's teeth to pointy knives. The reader can infer the knives are sharp and dangerous, just like the dog's teeth.

In order to understand text, you sometimes need to figure out the figurative language. Try the following steps:

1. What two things are being compared?

   ----

2. How are these two things similar?

   ----

3. What conclusion can you draw from this comparison?

   After the hurricane, the backyard was a lake.

   The backyard is not really a lake. This is a metaphor. First, what is being compared?

   ------------------------ and ------------------------

   How are these two things similar?

   What conclusion can you draw from this comparison?

- You should have said the backyard and a lake were being compared.
- They are similar because they are both big puddles of standing water.
- I can conclude that the hurricane deposited a lot of water and now the backyard is flooded.

Answering Multiple-Choice Questions

After reading the passage, you will be faced with the multiple-choice or text-based questions. Again, you may be tempted to read these questions before you read the story. DO NOT DO THIS! If you read the questions first, you are going to be looking for the answers and not paying attention to ALL of the text. You will need to understand ALL of the text in order to construct the essay. Again, the only question you *should* read is the essay question. This allows you to mark evidence, as you read. Next, read the passage carefully and use your reading strategies. Then, when you get to the multiple-choice questions, you will be prepared. Read the hints for answering multiple-choice questions, and then you'll have a chance to practice.

HINTS FOR MULTIPLE-CHOICE QUESTIONS

> Mark key words in both the question and answers. You are allowed to highlight on the test and often it helps!

> Read the entire question and ALL of the answer choices. Make sure your choice is answering the question. Often, the wrong choices are also from the text and look correct. Just because you recognize the sentence, doesn't mean it is correct!

> Use the process of elimination. Cross off answers that you know are incorrect.

> Answer EVERY question. Make a logical guess if you don't know the answer.

> Use all of your time! Check your answers carefully when you are done. During the real test, you should not be the first to finish. If you are done before everyone else, you MUST go back through the section and check all work.

Let's Practice

Reread the story from earlier in the chapter. Then, answer each multiple-choice and text-based question.

"The Look"

1 As I sauntered through the front door, I saw my mom standing in the foyer, her arms crossed, and the look I knew all too well on her face. It was the look that most mom's mastered early on in your childhood, the look that let you know to knock it off or else. The worst-case scenario was walking through the front door and seeing that look waiting for you. I knew immediately I was in for it.

2 "Uh, hi Mom. How are you?" I asked forcing my big brown eyes to become even bigger and using my most innocent voice. Mom didn't answer. Instead, she just stared at me, shaking her head. She was a lioness ready to pounce, and I just needed to figure out which antic she found out about. I was pretty sure she couldn't have found out about the mall, but maybe it was what happened in math class.

3 "Would you like to explain this, Connor?" Mom said as she waved an envelope between the two of us. "I don't understand why you keep getting into all this trouble." She continued to shout as the paper jabbed back and forth. She looked like a knight trying to slay the evil dragon.

4 I could tell from the envelope it had been mailed from Wilson Elementary School. I had erased the message on the machine from my math teacher and the one from the principal, too. I guess they finally mailed a letter home explaining why I had in-school suspension last week. I had to think fast. Maybe I could still get out of this.

5 "I can explain, Mom," I quickly said. What now? How could I justify shooting spitballs at Jessica Johnson? Then I blurted out, "I didn't do it!" As soon as the words flew out of my mouth I wanted to take them back. I knew I shouldn't have said it, but I couldn't help myself. Now I was really in for it. "It was RJ! He sits next to me, and the teacher made a mistake. I didn't want to rat him out." I didn't know what was wrong with me. The lies were lava flowing from an active volcano. There was no stopping them.

6 "I'll take care of this immediately," my mom said with a sympathetic look on her face. Before I could protest, she picked up the phone and started to dial. I slunk into the chair, mortified, but not knowing what to say. I knew RJ's mom wouldn't believe him and he would be grounded for a month. I listened to my mom retell the story. Then she said the dreaded words. "I'm just disappointed that RJ let Connor get in trouble for something he did." I couldn't take it any longer.

7 "Stop, Mom! I did it! I was sitting behind Jessica and I was angry that she had gotten an A on the test. I thought it would be funny to shoot spitballs into her hair. She would leave the room with all the tiny pieces of paper stuck in her head and people would laugh. It was wrong! I know it was wrong!"

8 At that moment, my mom hung up the phone without saying another word. She had a knowing smile on her face and she said in a very calm voice, "Go to your room." It was at that moment that I realized my mom was smarter than I thought. She knew all along I was lying. She had never dialed RJ's mom and I had admitted everything. All I could do was accept the <u>consequence</u>. I knew I deserved whatever punishment she gave me and I was sure it would be a big one.

1. Part A. In the last paragraph, it states, "All I could do was accept the consequence." What does consequence mean in this sentence?

- ○ a. To get caught
- ○ b. Cause
- ○ c. Reward for past behavior
- ○ d. Outcome or result of something that happened earlier

Part B. Which phrase best helps the reader understand the meaning of consequence?

- ○ a. *My mom was smarter than I thought.*
- ○ b. *She had a knowing smile on her face.*
- ○ c. *I knew I deserved whatever punishment she gave me.*
- ○ d. *She knew all along I was lying.*

2. Part A. In the story the narrator describes his mom as "a lioness ready to pounce." This is an example of

- ○ a. simile.
- ○ b. metaphor.
- ○ c. personification.
- ○ d. alliteration.

Part B. What can you infer from the figurative language?

- ○ a. Mom is angry and ready to grill him as soon as he enters the house.
- ○ b. Mom is angry, but she doesn't look it, yet.
- ○ c. Mom is very hungry.
- ○ d. Mom likes cats.

3. **Part A.** At the end of paragraph 6, Connor says, "I couldn't take it any longer." Which part of the story structure does this represent?

"I'll take care of this immediately," my mom said with a sympathetic look on her face. Before I could protest, she picked up the phone and started to dial. I slunk into the chair, mortified, but not knowing what to say. I knew RJ's mom wouldn't believe him and he would be grounded for a month. I listened to my mom retell the story. Then she said the dreaded words. "I'm just disappointed that RJ let Connor get in trouble for something he did." I couldn't take it any longer.

- O a. The problem
- O b. The turning point
- O c. The resolution
- O d. The rising action

Part B. Underline the detail that best supports your answer from Part A.

4. **Part A.** Which sentence best states the theme of the story?

- O a. Do your homework and get good grades.
- O b. Do not lie because it will get you in trouble.
- O c. Being sneaky pays off.
- O d. Be nice to others.

Part B. Which paragraph from the story best supports your answer in Part A?

- O a. Paragraph 1
- O b. Paragraph 2
- O c. Paragraph 4
- O d. Paragraph 8

Answers are on page 157.

Prose Constructed Response

You may be asked to analyze the literature by answering a question with a written response. Analyze simply means to look closely at each part of the text in order to figure it out or explain it. Often, the prose constructed response will be based on two reading passages. For this example, we will use just one article and focus on the structure of the essay. When you practice independently, you will have two texts to read and analyze.

Your prose constructed response will be scored using a 0–4 point rubric. Take a minute and look at the elements of the rubric.

1. **Reading**—Comprehension of the key ideas
   - ☐ Response answers the question.
   - ☐ Response provides accurate analysis of the text.
   - ☐ Response shows clear understanding of the text.
   - ☐ Response makes inferences based on the text.
   - ☐ Response references the text (uses proof from the story).
   - ☐ Response explains the evidence in a clear and meaningful way.

2. **Written Expression**—Development of ideas, organization, and clarity of language
   - ☐ Response addresses the prompt. (Did you do what the prompt tells you to do?)
   - ☐ Response is clear and detailed.
   - ☐ Response stays on topic.
   - ☐ Response makes sense.
   - ☐ The introduction is strong.
   - ☐ The closing is strong.
   - ☐ Response uses transitions.

3. **Writing**—Knowledge of language and conventions

- ☐ Writing is well edited to avoid errors.
- ☐ Sentences are complete.
- ☐ Punctuation is used properly.
- ☐ Words are spelled correctly.

When completing the essay, you will need to keep three things in mind: introduce, support, and conclude. Introduce simply means to restate the question or prompt, establish your background, and make it clear what the essay will be about. Read the sample below to see how to restate the question.

Question:

- How was Connor feeling when his Mom was on the phone with RJ's mom?
- What does this tell us about Connor?

Use evidence from the text to support your answer.

Introduce: Throughout "The Look" the reader learns a lot about the main character, Connor. Although he is dishonest and lies to his mom, he later shows that he has some integrity. When Connor's mom is on the phone with RJ's mom, there is evidence that Connor feels guilty about the situation. However, the reader also learns that he cares about his friends and has a surprising innocence when he believes his mom's lie.

Within this paragraph, the author must restate the question. Simply turn the question into a statement by taking out the asking words. "Guilty" could be replaced with another word of your choice, as long as you have evidence from the text to support your idea.

Next, you will need to support your answer. This can be done in just a couple of paragraphs, but you must have evidence from the text. For example, in the story Connor feels guilty. The reader knows this because he slunk into the chair, mortified, and he interrupted his mom when she voiced her disappointment. This is the evidence I will use when I write my essay. I will also need to explain how this evidence proves my point.

Because this is a two-part question, I will need to restate the second part. For example, I might say, "This tells me that Connor is a good friend to RJ." Again, I'll need to look for support in the text. Any time you are writing about text, you *must* include proof from the story or article. Perhaps I can talk about how Connor admitted he lied because he "knew RJ's mom wouldn't believe him and he would be grounded for a month." If Connor didn't care about RJ, he wouldn't have told the truth and, instead, he would have let RJ get into trouble.

This situation also shows the reader that Connor is a little innocent or gullible. When Connor's mom "calls" RJ's mom, she easily tricks Connor into telling the truth. He is unable to recognize that she is now lying to him. This may backfire later because she is not teaching that lying is wrong in this situation.

Finally, the author needs to conclude the essay. This means that the author summarizes his or her thoughts and wraps up the essay in an interesting way.

Throughout the writing, an author uses transition words to help the writing sound fluent. Sophisticated transition words will enhance your writing. Use the following chart to help you:

First Evidence Transitions	As proof of this; In fact; For example; For instance; In support of this
Additional Evidence Transitions	Furthermore; Likewise; Additionally; Moreover
Explanation Transitions	Therefore; Hence; Thus; This means; As a result
Conclusion Transitions	Therefore; Hence; Thus; In conclusion; In brief

Now let's read the response below. In this answer the author introduces his or her ideas, supports the idea with evidence from the text, and concludes by summarizing the essay.

Throughout "The Look" the reader learns a lot about the main character, Connor. Although he is dishonest and lies to his mom, he later shows that he has some integrity. When Connor's mom is on the phone with RJ's mom, there is evidence that Connor feels guilty about the situation. However, the reader also learns that he cares about his friends and has a surprising innocence when he believes his mom's lie.

In fact, in the story, it says, "I (Connor) slunk into the chair, mortified, but not knowing what to say. I knew RJ's mom wouldn't believe him and he would be grounded for a month." Hence, Connor doesn't like what his mom is saying and it's probably because he knows it's not true. If a person lies and gets caught, often he or she feels bad or guilty about the situation. If Connor didn't feel guilty, he would simply sit back, listen, and let RJ take the fall. Furthermore, when his mom says she's disappointed in RJ, Connor breaks down and admits the truth. He doesn't want his friend to get in trouble for something he did. This proves that Connor was feeling guilty about what happened. Otherwise, he wouldn't have admitted the truth.

This situation shows a couple of things about Connor. First, it proves that he is actually a good friend to RJ. He "knew RJ's mom wouldn't believe him and he would be grounded for a month." If Connor didn't care about RJ, he wouldn't have told the truth and, instead, he would have let RJ get into trouble. Furthermore, it shows Connor is gullible. This means he believes people. When Connor's mom "calls" RJ's mom, she easily tricks Connor into telling the truth. He is unable to recognize that she is now lying to him.

In conclusion, the story depicts Connor as dishonest, yet the reader can also see that he is a good friend. He has some positive characteristics even though he is mean when he throws a spitball and dishonest when he lies to his mom.

Take a minute to read the following hints. Then, you will practice this part of the test by reading two different passages, answering questions, and constructing an essay.

Practice Time!

Now it is your turn to practice! The PARCC will probably give you two passages and ask you to answer questions and write a written response using both stories or articles. This is where you will analyze the text.

Make sure you read the directions carefully. The practice will give you a variety of questions. There may not be so many on the actual PARCC and you will see fewer in the practice test at the back of the book. Good luck, and remember to use all the hints you have learned so far! You may use highlighters or your pencil to mark your text, as needed. When you are finished, check your answers in the back of the book.

HINTS FOR SUCCESS

- Do not read the multiple-choice questions before reading the story! Even though you might be tempted, you will need to read carefully in order to understand the entire text. You don't want to be tempted to just look for answers.
- You should read the prose constructed response question. As you read, mark evidence that will support your response.
- Slow down! It will benefit you to read using your strategies! Mentally interact with the text. Ask questions and make predictions. Then, read to see if you are right or wrong. Remember, your goal is to read and understand the text the FIRST time!
- Remember to restate it, support it, and conclude it when answering your prose constructed response. You MUST use evidence from the text! Quote your proof by finding evidence and copying it word for word. Make sure you use quotation marks and, if there are two articles, to say which author or article made the statement.
- Apply strategies for answering multiple-choice questions. Read the entire question and all of the options. Eliminate possibilities that you know are wrong.
- Answer every question!

Directions: Read each story and answer the questions. Then, construct a written response using evidence from both texts.

A Night to Remember

1 Abby collapsed onto the ground, her body shaking and loud sobs escaping into the still night. How had she gotten herself into this mess? After several minutes, she picked herself up and leaned against the tree behind her. The rough bark scraped against her back, reminding her of the disastrous situation. She stared up at the canopy of branches; the last tears sliding down her face. Someone had to be out there searching.

2 She turned her head to the right and listened intently. Then, she turned her head to the left and did the same thing. Her ears only found silence, but then she heard leaves rustling from behind. Abby's heart skipped a beat and she jumped to her feet with a big smile on her face. "I'm over here!" she yelled loudly. At that moment, she realized it wasn't Mrs. Watts, her scout leader, or one of the other girls from her troop, rustling the leaves. She was just hearing a lone deer searching for food in the dense forest. Abby burst into tears one more time and the frightened doe took off into the dark woods.

3 Just two hours ago, Abby was having fun with all her friends in Troop 524. The ten girls had just arrived at Camp Bernie with their scout leader, Mrs. Watts, and Jenna's mom, Mrs. Johnson. The first thing they did was set up camp. The girls unloaded the heavy equipment and began working together to get the tents up and the trucks unloaded. Abby wasn't happy about any of it. "This is hard work," she complained to her best friend Jenna. "I shouldn't be sweating. This is supposed to be a vacation, right?"

4 Jenna stared at Abby with a slightly confused look on her face. "It won't take us too long," Jenna finally replied as she started to secure the tent to the stakes. Jenna camped with her family at least once a month and as she worked the smile returned to her face.

5 "I know. I just thought we were going to have more fun on this trip," Abby complained as she kicked at the dirt. Abby was eleven years old, but this was her first time camping and it was nothing like she imagined.

6 After the girls set up the tents, it was time to start gathering firewood. They needed a fire to cook food and stay warm at night. "Everyone stick with at least one friend," Mrs. Watts instructed the girls, "and don't wander too far!" Eager to get started, the troop set off in groups of two or three girls.

7 At first, Abby headed off with her two best friends, Jenna and Tiffany. They found a few large branches, and Jenna and Tiffany both had their arms full. Then, Abby saw a really cool grouping of rocks just up the hill. It looked like the perfect place to plop down and relax in the sun. I'll check it out first and then tell Jenna and Tiffany, Abby thought. It can be our secret hangout while we're camping this weekend. Abby started heading up the hill towards the cluster of rocks. She had to keep looking down to make sure she didn't fall and after a while, when she looked up, the rocks were nowhere to be found. I thought I was heading right towards them, she thought to herself.

8 Now, here she was, alone and crying in the woods. The sun was starting to set and the temperature was quickly dropping. Abby didn't know what to do. She thought back to what Mrs. Watts always told them in scouts, "If you ever get lost, you should stay in one place."

9 Abby knew what she had to do, but it was getting cold and she had no fire. I'll try to gather some branches to use as shelter, she thought to herself. For about an hour, Abby worked hard to lean branches and leaves between two trees. She layered as many leaves on the ground as she could and then settled herself in to wait for someone to find her.

10 As the sun set, she heard rustling behind her again. Only this time she also heard sniffing and scratching. Abby froze, her eyes wide. She heard the rustling getting closer. Her hands began to sweat, despite the cold temperatures, and an uneasy feeling swirled around her stomach. Don't move, and it will go away, Abby thought to herself as she clenched her big eyes shut and became a statue in the middle of the dark forest. After what seemed like a millennium, the sounds started to drift further and further away. A sigh of relief escaped Abby's chest, she took a few deep breaths before feeling her shoulders ease. Thoughts raced through her mind. How did I get myself into this mess? Why wasn't I paying attention? I never should have left the girls!

11 It was at that moment that Abby saw a dull light far in the distance. Could it be a flashlight? Abby took a chance and began yelling, "Help, I'm over here!" The lights began to get closer and closer. Abby jumped to her feet. It was really happening. Someone was coming to save her. Just then Mrs. Watts, Jenna, and Tiffany appeared from behind a tree. Rivulets of tears ran down Abby's face and she sprinted toward them.

12 When she reached her scout leader and friends, she threw her cold body into their arms and squeezed with all her strength. "I'm so sorry," she said. "I didn't mean to disappear. It was an accident." She tried to catch her breath but she was crying so hard it was difficult to talk.

13 "I'm glad you're OK, but I hope you learned your lesson, Abby," Mrs. Watts said with a slight scowl on her face. As she hugged Abby back, a small breath escaped Mrs. Watts lips and her shoulders finally relaxed.

14 "It won't happen again. I promise," Abby said sincerely.

15 When the group returned to camp, dinner was ready and waiting for them. As the meal ended, Abby jumped up and quickly said, "I'll do all the dishes." Before anyone could oppose, she collected the plates and began cleaning up. Maybe camping wasn't so bad after all.

Choose the best answer for each question.

1. **Part A.** In paragraph 2, Abby listens intently. Intently means

- ○ a. with great attention.
- ○ b. quietly.
- ○ c. with anticipation.
- ○ d. with hope.

Part B. Underline the two most substantial sentences that justify your answer for Part A.

She turned her head to the right and listened intently. Then, she turned her head to the left and did the same thing. Her ears only found silence, but then she heard leaves rustling from behind. Abby's heart skipped a beat and she jumped to her feet with a big smile on her face. "I'm over here!" she yelled loudly. At that moment, she realized it wasn't Mrs. Watts, her scout leader, or one of the other girls from her troop, rustling the leaves. She was just hearing a lone deer searching for food in the dense forest. Abby burst into tears one more time and the frightened doe took off into the dark woods.

2. **Part A.** The metaphor *Abby was a statue* means that Abby was

- ○ a. still.
- ○ b. tough.
- ○ c. strong.
- ○ d. scared.

Part B. Which detail provides support for your answer to Part A?

- ○ a. As the sun set, she heard rustling behind her again.
- ○ b. The sounds started to drift further and further away.
- ○ c. Her hands began to sweat, despite the cold temperatures, and an uneasy feeling swirled around her stomach.
- ○ d. Abby froze, her eyes wide.

3. **Part A.** How does this sentence from paragraph 11 help develop the plot of the story?

   It was at that moment that Abby saw a dull light far in the distance.

   ○ a. It represents the conflict, or problem.
   ○ b. It represents the turning point.
   ○ c. It represents the resolution.
   ○ d. It represents the rising action.

   Part B. Which detail best supports your answer for Part A?

   ○ a. *Could it be a flashlight?*
   ○ b. *Abby jumped to her feet.*
   ○ c. *Just then Mrs. Watts, Jenna, and Tiffany appeared from behind a tree.*
   ○ d. *Someone was coming to save her.*

4. **Part A.** How are the events of paragraphs 3, 4, and 5 important to the theme?

   ○ a. They show that Abby is not happy about the hard work necessary for camping.
   ○ b. They show that Abby is a good friend to all the girls in her troop.
   ○ c. They show that Abby is unhappy and doesn't want to be in the woods.
   ○ d. They show that Abby doesn't like her troop and would rather be home.

   Part B. Which detail best supports the idea in Part A?

   ○ a. *Abby was eleven years old, but this was her first time camping…*
   ○ b. *Jenna stared at Abby with a slightly confused look on her face.*
   ○ c. *Just two hours ago, Abby was having fun with all her friends in Troop 524.*
   ○ d. *"This is hard work," she complained to her best friend Jenna. "I shouldn't be sweating."*

Answers are on page 158.

Now you will read Aesop's fable, "The Ant and The Grasshopper." You will answer a few questions about this story and then respond in writing to a question.

The Ant and the Grasshopper

An Aesop Fable

1 In a field one summer's day, a Grasshopper was hopping about, chirping and singing to its heart's content. An Ant passed by, bearing along with great toil an ear of corn he was taking to the nest.

2 "Why not come and chat with me," said the Grasshopper, "instead of toiling and moiling in that way?"

3 "I am helping to lay up food for the winter," said the Ant, "and recommend you to do the same."

4 "Why bother about winter?" said the Grasshopper; we have got plenty of food at present." But the Ant went on its way and continued its toil. When the winter came the Grasshopper had no food and found itself dying of hunger, while it saw the ants distributing every day corn and grain from the stores they had collected in the summer. Then the Grasshopper knew:

5 *Moral of Aesop's Fable: It is best to prepare for the days of necessity.*

1. **Part A.** What is the meaning of the word toil as it is used in paragraphs 1 and 2?

   - O a. Heavy
   - O b. Hard work
   - O c. Hungry
   - O d. Easy work

   Part B. Which detail from the story provides the best clue for the meaning of toil?

   - O a. *"Why not come and chat with me," said the Grasshopper, "instead of toiling and moiling in that way?"*
   - O b. *In a field one summer's day a Grasshopper was hopping about, chirping and singing to its heart's content.*
   - O c. *"I am helping to lay up food for the winter," said the Ant, "and recommend you to do the same."*
   - O d. *Grasshopper had no food, and found itself dying of hunger.*

2. **Part A.** Which statement best expresses a theme from the story?

   - O a. Balance work and fun for a happy life.
   - O b. Work together.
   - O c. Hard work pays off.
   - O d. Listen to other's advice.

   Part B. Which detail from the story provides the best evidence for the answer to A?

   - O a. *"Why not come and chat with me," said the Grasshopper, "instead of toiling and moiling in that way?"*
   - O b. *"Why bother about winter?" said the Grasshopper; we have got plenty of food at present."*
   - O c. *In a field one summer's day a Grasshopper was hopping about, chirping and singing to its heart's content.*
   - O d. *When the winter came the Grasshopper had no food and found itself dying of hunger, while it saw the ants distributing every day corn and grain from the stores they had collected in the summer.*

3. Choose from the sentences below to create a summary of the text. Choose three sentences that describe key events. Label the first event 1, the second 2, and the third 3. Cross out the two you are not including in your summary.

The ant carried an ear of corn.	
Grasshopper tries to get Ant to stop working and talk to him, but Ant keeps working.	
When winter comes, Grasshopper doesn't have enough food but the ants do.	
Ant advises Grasshopper to work hard to collect food, but Grasshopper doesn't listen.	
Grasshopper was hopping and singing across the field.	

Answers are on page 158.

Prose Constructed Response

You just read two stories, "A Night to Remember" and "The Ant and the Grasshopper." How are the main characters from each story similar and different. Use evidence from the text to support your answer.

Planning: Before you start writing think about how the characters are the same and how they are different. Use the space below for planning.

Use the checklist to assess your essay.

- [ ] I planned my essay before I started writing.
- [ ] My essay is at least four paragraphs long.
- [ ] I have an introduction paragraph with a thesis statement.
- [ ] My body paragraphs use evidence from each text.
- [ ] I explained each evidence in detail.
- [ ] I used appropriate transition words.
- [ ] I have a conclusion that wraps everything up and restates my thesis statement.

Answers are on page 159.

CHAPTER 4

Narrative Writing

Use the checklist to keep track of your work in this chapter.

- [ ] What Is Narrative Writing?
- [ ] Generating Your Idea with Story Pie
- [ ] Practice Prewriting
- [ ] Opening Your Story
- [ ] Details, Details, Details
- [ ] Ending Your Story
- [ ] Hints for Success
- [ ] Practice Time!

What Is Narrative Writing?

Narrative writing is simply telling, or narrating, a story. On the PARCC, you will be asked to develop or continue a story based on a reading passage. This is nothing to worry about. In this chapter, you will learn tips and structures for writing a great story, and it will be as easy as pie! Once you know how to structure your story, you'll get to see how this can connect to your reading.

Generating Your Idea with Story Pie

The first step to writing a story is coming up with your idea. This will be based on the text. Story pie will help you keep track of the details. Good writing happens with good prewriting, so remember to take the first five minutes to really think your story through! Let's take a look at each slice of the story pie.

Story Pie

Every piece of the pie helps create a good story!

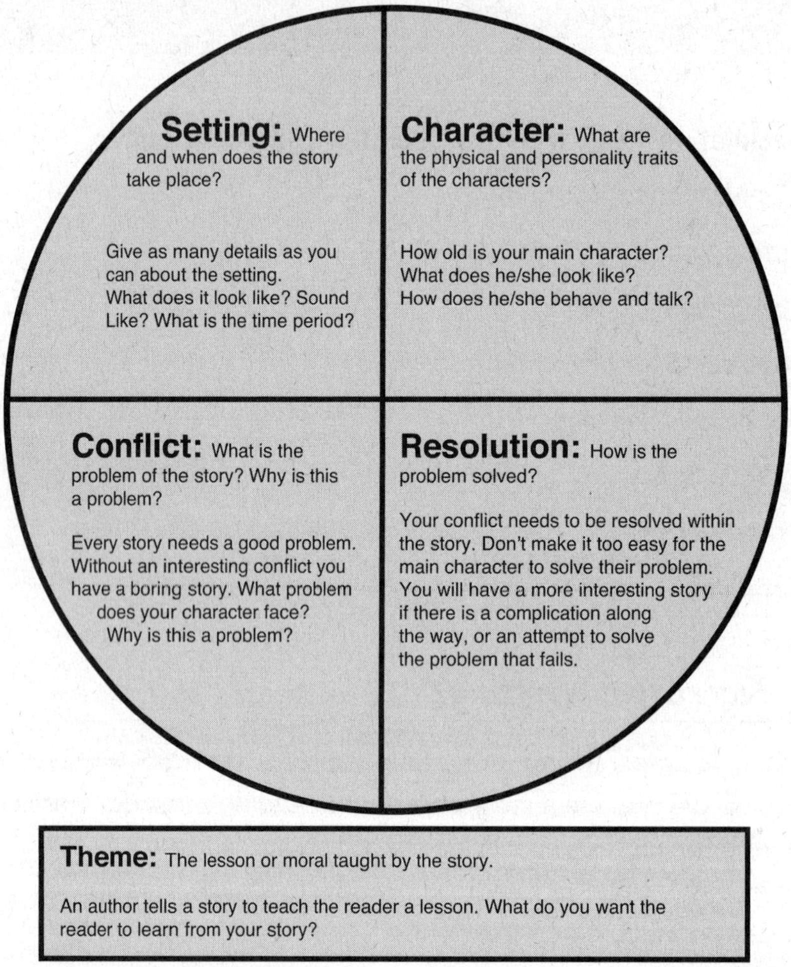

Story pie is quick to draw and allows you to think of the essential story elements *before* you begin writing. With this tool, prewriting will be as easy as pie!

The first slice is the setting. You want to have a good idea of when and where your story takes place. Think about the time period as well as the sensory details that surround your setting. Confused about sensory details? You have five senses—seeing, hearing, smelling, touching, and tasting. When an author writes descriptions focusing on the senses, it allows the reader to feel like they are a part of the story. It makes the writing vivid! When you are working on your prewrite, keep the sensory details in mind. Is it cold or hot and humid? Is it crowded or desolate?

The second slice of the pie describes your main character(s). Who is this story about? Really think about your character. Writing only a name is *not* good enough!

An author tells a story through the thoughts, words, and actions of his or her characters. In order to do this, you need to know your character. Write down physical and character traits. Physical traits will be what you character looks like. Character traits will be how the character behaves. Is he or she selfish, kind, or mean? You will need to have these things in mind when you give your character actions, words, and thoughts.

The conflict, or problem, is the third slice of the pie. *Every* story *must* have a problem. Often, with a narrative prompt you are given part of the problem, and you might just need to add more information. When you are writing the problem, you want it to be a significant problem. It can't be too simple to fix. You want your character to have to work a little to solve the problem. Otherwise, you will have a *boring* story. Make sure you also know *why* this is a problem for your character.

The final slice is the resolution, or solution to the problem. How will your conflict conclude? Again, this shouldn't be done too easily; otherwise, you don't have much of a story. If the problem is Joey lost his sock and the solution is he walked to the store and bought a new pair of socks, the reader is probably going to be completely bored. Who wants to read a story that isn't exciting? The reader wants to see the character have a challenge. This slice *must* include an attempt to solve the problem or a roadblock. Your character needs to try to solve the problem and have it not work for one reason or another.

All of these slices of pie sit upon the theme. What is the theme? The theme is the lesson the author would like to teach the reader. Every good story teaches a lesson. Think about the stories you have read or heard. You may have learned not to lie, to listen to your parents, or to be kind to others. All of these life lessons are themes. When you are writing your story, you will need to think about the lesson you want the reader to learn.

Look at the following story example to see how story pie can help you find the ingredients for a successful piece of writing! For our purposes, we will simply be working on story structure. When you get to the practice prompt, it will be based on a reading passage, just like the PARCC.

Let's assume you just read a story about Emily's family going on a vacation. In the story Emily forgot to pack something really important. You probably answered a few questions about the story and now are faced with a writing prompt.

Narrative Prompt

Write a story about how the missing item effects Emily on her vacation. Use what you know about the setting and characters when writing your story.

Story Pie

Every piece of the pie helps create a good story!

Setting: Where and when does the story take place?

Present time
Month of May
Williamsburg, Virginia

Character: What are the physical and personality traits of the characters?

Emily is eleven years old. She is stubborn and gets angry when she doesn't get her way. Emily has brown hair and brown eyes.

Conflict: What is the problem of the story?

Emily left her writing journal at home.

Why is it a problem?

Since she is missing school, her teacher told her she must keep a journal of her trip and record what she learns. Her family is only going to the amusement park, once her work is done.

Resolution: How is the problem solved?

Emily's parents ask if she has done her work. Emily lies and says it is done. When her parents ask to see it, Emily tries to trick them. It doesn't work. She's forced to tell the truth. Her parents are angry but together they figure out a video solution. Emily realizes it would have been easier to tell the truth in the beginning.

Theme: What lesson or moral would you like to teach the reader?

It is easier to be honest and tell the truth.

After completing this quick prewrite, it will be easy to write a detailed story.

Practice Prewriting

Now it's your turn! What will Emily forget in your story? Use the organizer to help you plan and practice story writing.

Story Pie

Every piece of the pie helps create a good story!

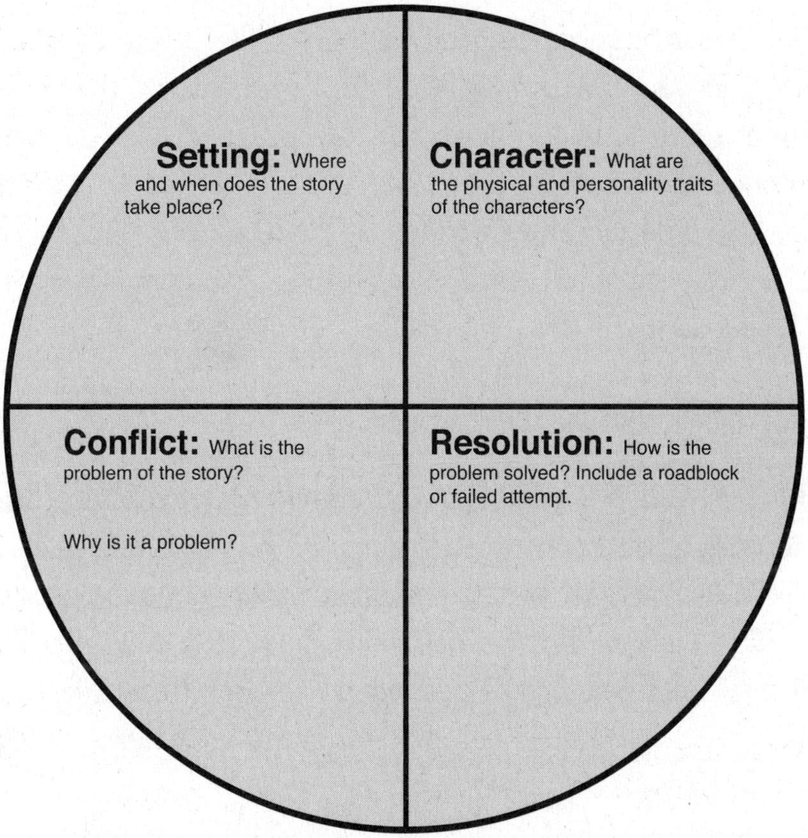

Theme: What lesson or moral would you like to teach the reader?

Opening Your Story

Once you've finished your prewrite, it's time to draft. One of the easiest ways to make the reader want to read your story is to have a gripping opening, or lead. You can do this in many different ways! You'll need to experiment a little to find out what works for you.

An easy way to begin is to start off with the character thinking, saying, or doing something. Perhaps Emily might be thinking at the beginning of our story:

> Mom and Dad are going to ground me for life! I must have left that dumb journal sitting on my bed. Emily sat in the middle of the hotel room with her suitcase dumped out around her. Her journal was the one thing she REALLY needed to pack for this trip. Not only were her grades at risk but her trip to ride Mountain Adventure at the Great Virginia Amusement Park was also in jeopardy.

Or maybe we should start with Emily in action:

> Emily dumped out her suitcase and searched frantically. She threw her new pink bathing suit across the room followed by her yellow sundress and the matching flip-flops. She tore through each piece of clothes before burying her face into the pillow of the hotel bed. Tears poured out of her brown eyes. "Forgetting that journal is going to ruin my vacation," Emily mumbled to herself.

Another way to begin your story is with a vivid description. If you use this strategy, you will want to focus on the sensory details. What does the setting look like, sound like, or feel like?

Let's look at our story about Emily one last time:

> As Emily stared out the window, she focused on the mountainous roller coaster ahead of her. The bright, yellow car slowly crept up the never-ending hill and she could faintly hear the clicking in the distance. Just as the car flew down the steep

hill, it hit her. She might not ever get to ride this incredible roller coaster because she had made a HUGE mistake! She had forgotten to pack the one thing she needed most on this trip to Williamsburg, Virginia.

Practice Opening Your Story

Now it's your turn. Look back at your own prewriting for this story. How will you grab the reader's attention and start your story? Use the space below to practice.

I will begin with

- [ ] the character speaking
- [ ] the character thinking
- [ ] the character in action
- [ ] a vivid description

Details, Details, Details

As you develop your story, you will want to include detailed sentences. By adding adjectives and adverbs you can create a more descriptive piece of writing. What is the job of an adjective? An adjective describes a noun. For example, "roller coaster" is a noun. If I wanted to describe this roller coaster I would need to use adjective like "tall," "fast," "scary," or "amazing." An adverb has the same job as an adjective, only it describes a verb. For example, if I wanted to describe how Emily looked for the journal in her suitcase, I could say she frantically looked, desperately looked, or quickly looked. "Frantically," "desperately," and "quickly" are my adverbs. They all describe the verb "looked."

In addition to great word choice, an author wants to make the reader feel like a character in the story. How are you going to do this? Show, don't tell techniques are your answer! Show, don't tell simply means that you want to describe what is happening in the scene. For example, instead of just saying Emily was upset, we can say Emily slouched back onto the bed defeated. The tears began to pour out of her eyes as she held her head in her hands. Now, we've *shown* how Emily is feeling rather than just saying she's sad. It's your turn to give this a try.

Let's revise some simple, boring sentences into more descriptive sentences. Read each of the sentences below. Then, try to add adjectives and adverbs to make them more vivid. Keep word choice in mind as you revise. Are there more sophisticated or meaningful words to use? Remember, you want to show, not tell the details. Look at the example below:

Original Writing

Emily ran toward the roller coaster. She was nervous and excited.

Revised Writing

Emily sprinted toward the huge roller coaster. Her smile filled her face, and she could feel her heart beating in her chest. As she reached the line, Emily looked up at the steep hill above her and felt the flutters in her stomach.

Practice Adding Details

Read each sentence. Then revise for better word choice and to add details.

Emily looked through her suitcase for the journal.

Emily walked into her parents' room and admitted she forgot her journal at home.

Maybe the middle of your story will look something like this:

What was she going to do? Emily was missing school to go on this trip with her family, and she had to do her work before she was allowed to go to the amusement park. Her teacher gave Emily a journal to write down everything that happened to her on the trip. How was she going to do her work if she didn't have the journal?

"Emily?" Emily's mom called from the other room of the hotel.

"Yes, Mom?" Emily replied nervously.

Emily's mom asked, "Did you finish the first part of your journal? We are almost ready to go to the park."

What was Emily going to do? She didn't do her work. She was going to ruin the vacation for everyone.

"I just finished, Mom," Emily said, panicked.

"Good, bring it in here and let me see it," her mom answered.

Oh, no! What was Emily going to do? She lied and now she was going to get caught. She grabbed the notebook from the hotel desk and walked over to her parents.

"See it's right here," she quickly said as she waved it around. "All done. No need to check the work." Just when she thought she was in the clear, her mom put out her hand. **This isn't going to work, she thought to herself. I should just tell the truth.**

Emily walked over to her parents and told them that she forgot her journal at home and then she lied so she didn't ruin everyone's vacation. While she was crying, she said she was sorry about one million times. Emily's parents told her to go sit down while they talked about her punishment for lying.

"We are so disappointed in you for lying, Emily. Everyone forgets sometimes, and this wouldn't have been a big deal if you were honest from the beginning." Emily sat anxiously waiting for the verdict. "As your punishment, we will be leaving one day early."

Emily was very upset, but she understood now that what she did was wrong. She asked her parents for help. Her father looked at his video camera and said, "I have an idea." The three of them spent the rest of the day walking around with the video camera, acting like colonists, and explaining the historical buildings and sites of Williamsburg. In the end, Emily learned a lot and had a great time. Now that work was out of the way, it was time to hit the park.

Remember, tell your story through actions, words, and thoughts. To review how to write engaging dialogue, go to Chapter 5.

Ending Your Story

Ending your story is critical on this part of the test. You must finish the story in order to maximize your score. This means that you must resolve the conflict or solve the problem. Often, you can end the story in a similar way to your opening. You can have the character speaking, thinking, or being involved in an action. Sometimes, an author will write a circular ending. In this type of ending, the author revisits the lead. Remember, endings are important to the story! You want to have impact on the reader with your final words.

In our story about Emily, she has forgotten her journal, which she needs for her school assignment, at home. In order for Emily to go to the amusement park, she must first complete her assignment about historic Williamsburg. Unfortunately, this is impossible without the journal. At first, Emily lies to her parents but later admits that she has not done her work. Emily's parents are angry and Emily cries. She asks them to help her solve this problem. Together, Emily and her parents decide to make a video journal of their trip. They have fun performing and describing the historic sites. At the end, Emily makes it to the amusement park and rides the roller coaster she had been waiting for.

How can we write an exciting closing for this story? Let's look at a few examples. The first idea would be to end with an action, such as Emily riding down the roller coaster.

> Emily's long hair flew behind her as she catapulted down the huge hill of Mountain Adventure. She could barely contain the excitement as she threw her arms in the air and let out a loud scream. Her smile stretched across her entire face as she thought to herself, I sure am lucky to be here. Then it slowly started to disappear, as she realized she could have been at the park for an extra day if she had just been honest with her parents from the start.

A circular ending might work if we revisit the scene of Emily with her suitcase. Reread the opening from earlier:

> Emily frantically dumped her suitcase out. She threw her new pink bathing suit across the room, followed by her yellow sundress and the matching flip-flops. She tore through each piece of clothes before burying her face into the pillow of the

hotel bed. Tears poured out of her brown eyes. "Forgetting that journal is going to ruin my vacation," Emily mumbled to herself.

Now, let's try an ending:

Emily slowly folded her clothes and put them back into the suitcase. First her new pink bathing suit, which wasn't so new anymore, then the yellow sundress and matching flip-flops. She thought back to the fun she had with her parents as they acted like the Colonists of Williamsburg and of the excitement of Mountain Adventure. "Forgetting that journal didn't ruin my vacation," Emily said to herself as she proudly held her videotape journal. "It just slowed me down a little."

Practice Ending Your Story

It's your turn! Look back at your story plan. How might you end the story? Will you make Emily involved in an action? Maybe you'll use dialogue or have Emily thinking. Perhaps you'll even try a circular ending!

I will end with

- ☐ the character speaking
- ☐ the character thinking
- ☐ the character in action
- ☐ a circular ending

Now it is your turn to practice. On the following pages, you will find two sample writing prompts. Space is left after the prompt to draw and fill in your own pie chart. You then have four blank pages to write your story. Make sure you read the directions carefully and use what you have learned in this chapter.

HINTS FOR SUCCESS

- Prewrite! Prewrite! Prewrite! Planning your idea for a story will not only give you a place to begin but also show you how to finish. You have a limited time for each part of the test. When you do not prewrite, you will spend precious minutes trying to figure out where to go next.
- Start strong! Choose one of the four ways to begin your story: character thinking, character in action, character speaking, or a vivid description. Be clear and specific. Use your best vocabulary.
- Stay on topic! Stick to the plan. Make sure you stay with the problem of your story at all times. If Emily cannot find her journal, do not spend time telling the reader what souvenirs she wants to buy.
- Finish stronger! Choose one of the four ways to end your story: character thinking, character in action, character speaking, or a circular ending. Vivid descriptions and a clear resolution to the main character's problem will pack your story with a powerful punch.

When you finish writing the first prompt, read the sample story that follows. Also, read and use the rubric in the appendix so you can decide how your story will be scored. The rubric is what someone will use when they grade your writing on the PARCC. The scorer will read your writing and decide if you are a strong writer, a writer who is good but makes some mistakes, or a writer who needs more practice to create a good story. Plan your ideas, use your skills, and do your best! Good luck!

Practice Time!

The narrative task may be based on a passage you have read. In the last chapter, you analyzed "The Ant and the Grasshopper." Reread the short fable and then respond to the prompt beneath the text.

The Ant and the Grasshopper

An Aesop Fable

1 In a field one summer's day, a Grasshopper was hopping about, chirping and singing to its heart's content. An Ant passed by, bearing along with great toil an ear of corn he was taking to the nest.

2 "Why not come and chat with me," said the Grasshopper, "instead of toiling and moiling in that way?"

3 "I am helping to lay up food for the winter," said the Ant, "and recommend you to do the same."

4 "Why bother about winter?" said the Grasshopper; we have got plenty of food at present." But the Ant went on its way and continued its toil. When the winter came the Grasshopper had no food and found itself dying of hunger, while it saw the ants distributing every day corn and grain from the stores they had collected in the summer. Then the Grasshopper knew:

5 *Moral of Aesop's Fable: It is best to prepare for the days of necessity.*

Sample Prompt #1

Write a story about Grasshopper's following winter. Use your knowledge of his character and the setting to develop your story.

Remember, you need to take a few minutes to plan your story. Make sure you include a problem, an attempt to solve the problem or a roadblock, and a resolution.

Use the space below to create your own story pie planner. Then, write your narrative on the lined pages.

Take a look back at the story you wrote, and use the checklist below to help you evaluate your own writing.

How did you start your story? I started with

- [ ] my character thinking
- [ ] my character talking
- [ ] my character in action
- [ ] a descriptive scene

How about the middle of your story?

- [ ] I had good word choice.
- [ ] I used show, don't tell details.
- [ ] I attempted to solve the problem, but it failed or I had a roadblock.
- [ ] I used dialogue.

How did you end the story? I ended with

- [ ] my character thinking
- [ ] my character talking
- [ ] my character in action
- [ ] a descriptive scene
- [ ] A circular ending
- [ ] I solved my problem or brought the story to a resolution of some sort.

A sample story is on page 160.

Keep your checklist in mind as you try your next practice prompt. With a little more practice, you'll be writing great stories in no time!

Sample Prompt #2

In Chapter 3, you read "A Night to Remember" and "The Ant and the Grasshopper." Both of the main characters learned an important personal lesson. Write a story where a character experiences a life-changing lesson.

Use the first five minutes to plan out your ideas. Revise and edit when you are finished writing. Use the space below to create your own story pie planner. Then, write your narrative on the lined pages.

Take a look back at the story you wrote and use the checklist below to help you evaluate your own writing.

How did you start your story? I started with

- [ ] my character thinking
- [ ] my character talking
- [ ] my character in action
- [ ] a descriptive scene

How about the middle of your story?

- [ ] I had good word choice.
- [ ] I used show, don't tell details.
- [ ] I attempted to solve the problem, but it failed or I had a roadblock.
- [ ] I used dialogue.

How did you end the story? I ended with

- [ ] my character thinking
- [ ] my character talking
- [ ] my character in action
- [ ] a descriptive scene
- [ ] a circular ending
- [ ] the problem solved or the story resolved in some other way

A sample story is on page 162.

CHAPTER 5

Don't Get Caught . . .

Use the checklist to keep track of your work in this chapter.

- [ ] Sentence Structure
- [ ] Comma Review
- [ ] Homophone Mix-Ups
- [ ] Writing Interesting Dialogue
- [ ] Using I and Me

This chapter will help you avoid making common errors when writing your essays, stories, or short responses. This might be review or new information for you. Either way, take some time to make sure you don't get caught by these common errors.

Sentence Structure

To be a successful writer, you need to understand sentence structure. This is important because you will want to vary the types of sentences you use in order to create an interesting piece of writing. Let's start by identifying what forms a complete sentence. There are two parts to every sentence, the subject and the predicate. The subject is who or what the sentence is about, and the predicate is the action of the sentence.

Subject = Noun (person, place, thing)
Predicate = Verb (action, state of being)

Read the sentence below and identify the subject and the predicate.

The dog ran.

The subject is "The dog" because the sentence is about the dog. "Ran" is the predicate because this is the action of the dog. Note that "dog" is the noun and "ran" is the verb.

A common mistake is to write only a subject or only a predicate. If this happens, the author does not have a complete sentence but instead has a fragment. Look at the samples below.

The excited dog.

This is not a complete sentence because it only includes a subject. The reader knows the sentence is about an excited dog but doesn't know the action of the dog because the predicate is missing.

Ran through the field.

This is not a complete sentence. The reader knows that someone or something ran through the field, but the reader does not know who is doing this action. In this case, the subject is missing.

Let's Practice

In this exercise, you will practice writing complete sentences. Each sentence fragment below is missing either the subject or predicate. Fix each fragment and then check your answers in the back of the book.

1. The lonely boy.

----

2. The angry teacher.

----

3. Played video games for hours.

----

4. Announced he won the lottery.

Answers are on page 163.

Now, why is it important to understand subject and predicate? There are several different types of sentences, and in order to write them correctly, you'll need to understand the independent clause. An independent clause consists of a subject and predicate. It can stand alone or be part of a sentence. By this definition "The dog ran" is an independent clause. On the other hand, a dependent clause has a subject and predicate but cannot stand alone. It doesn't make sense unless it is attached to an independent clause.

Independent Clause (IC) = subject and predicate and can stand alone.

Dependent Clause (DC) = subject and predicate but cannot stand alone.

Look at the examples below:

The happy dog greeted his owner.

This is an independent clause because it has a subject and predicate and can stand alone.

When the happy dog saw his owner

This is a dependent clause. It has a subject and predicate but cannot stand alone. It is an incomplete thought. What did the dog do when he saw his owner? In order for this to make sense, the clause needs to be attached to an independent clause.

When the happy dog saw his owner, he wagged his tail.

Once the independent clause, "he wagged his tail," is added, the sentence makes sense and is complete.

A common error when writing sentences is to combine two independent clauses using only a comma. This is called a comma splice and can be fixed by making the two independent clauses separate sentences or by adding a conjunction such as "and," "but," or "so." Another solution is to make one independent clause into a dependent clause.

A second common error is to combine two independent clauses without any punctuation. This is called a run-on sentence. This mistake can also be fixed by separating the independent clauses into two sentences or by adding a comma and conjunction. Again, the author could make one independent clause a dependent clause. Take a look at the examples below.

Comma splice = combining two independent clauses with only a comma

The dog barked, he scared the little girl.

Run-on sentence = combining two independent clauses with no punctuation

The dog barked he scared the little girl.

Here are some techniques you can use to fix comma splices and run-on sentences.

Fix-it Technique 1: Form two sentences.

The dog barked. He scared the little girl.

Fix-it Technique 2: Combine the two independent clauses with a conjunction.

The dog barked, and he scared the little girl.

Fix-it Technique 3: Change one independent clause into a dependent clause.

When the dog barked, he scared the little girl.

In the third fix-it technique, the author made "The dog barked" into the dependent clause "When the dog barked." This is a dependent clause because it has a subject "dog" and an action or predicate "barked," but it cannot stand alone. By itself, the clause does not make sense. This type of strategy is the most sophisticated fix-it technique of the three. When practicing, try and apply this technique.

Let's Practice

Fix each comma splice or run-on sentence. Try to use each fix-it technique at least once. Then, check your answers in the back of the book.

1. Tyler dove for the ball, he made the third out.

2. Grace performed in the talent show she won first place.

3. My cat cuddled on the couch, he purred when I pet him.

4. Reed studied for her science test she aced it.

Answers are on page 164.

Successful authors vary the sentence structure in their writing. We're going to focus on three types of sentence structures. The first is called a simple sentence. A simple sentence consists of one independent clause. The second type of sentence is called a compound sentence and is formed with two independent clauses. The third is a complex sentence. This is a more sophisticated sentence to write because it consists of one independent clause and one or more dependent clauses.

Simple sentence = 1 independent clause
Compound sentence = 2 independent clauses
Complex sentence = 1 independent clause and 1 or more dependent clauses

Read the examples below.

Simple sentence: The playful puppy chased the ball.

Compound sentence: The playful puppy chased the ball, and then he napped on the couch.

Complex sentence: After the playful puppy chased the ball, he napped on the couch.

Let's Practice

It's your turn to try to write each type of sentence. Use the space below to write three sentences about your favorite hobby.

1. Simple Sentence

----

2. Compound Sentence

----

3. Complex Sentence

Answers are on page 165.

Comma Review

When you take the PARCC, you will be expected to correctly use the comma in several situations. Review the following comma rules (CCSS ELA 5.2). Then, you will have a chance to practice each comma rule.

- Use a comma to separate items in a series (CCSS ELA 5.2A). Example: For lunch I ate a sandwich, grapes, yogurt, and a cookie.
- Use a comma to separate an introductory element from the rest of the sentence (CCSS ELA 5.2B). Example: After you review, you will complete the practice section.
- Use a comma to set off the words *yes* and *no* (e.g., *Yes, thank you*), to set off a tag question from the rest of the sentence (e.g., *It's true, isn't it?*), and to indicate direct address (e.g., *Is that you, Steve?*). (CCSS ELA 5.2C)

Let's Practice

Correctly place the commas into the sentences. Then, check your answers in the back of the book.

1. In order to earn my allowance I need to clean my room walk the dog and empty the dishwasher.

2. Elizabeth do you like to listen to music after school?

3. Yes I do like to listen to music in my free time.

Answers are on page 165.

Homophone Mix-Ups

One of the most common mistakes young authors make is the misuse of homophones. A homophone is defined as one of two or more words that sound alike but have different meanings and spellings. For example, "ate" and "eight" sound alike, but one means to consume food and the other defines a number. As you WRITE, you need to be careful that you are using the RIGHT homophone. Review the following list of common homophones.

There (Adverb) At or in that place

Please wait over there.

They're Contraction of they are

They're going for ice cream after the game.

Their (Possessive adjective) Belonging to them

Sydney and Olivia put the books in their lockers.

To (Preposition) Toward

She went to the teacher and asked for extra help.

Too (Adverb) Also; more than enough

I have too many stuffed animals to fit in my room.

Two Number

He bought two bags of chips in the cafeteria.

Allowed (Past tense verb) Allow or permit

Avery's parents allowed her to attend the slumber party.

Aloud (Adverb) Vocally; with a loud voice

My dad reads aloud to me before bed.

Effect (Noun) Result or consequence of something

The effect of studying was earning an A on the test.

Affect (Verb) Change or influence someone or something

Mrs. Simpson, my fourth grade teacher, affected my life because she taught me to believe in myself.

Threw (Past tense verb) Throw

The quarterback threw the ball for a touchdown.

Through (Preposition) Passing from one place to another

The player kicked the ball through the goal post.

Weather (Noun) State of the atmosphere in regards to temperature, precipitation

The weather was cold and rainy.

Whether (Conjunction) Used to indicate a single alternative

I need to decide whether to buy a Honda or Toyota.

Plain (Adjective) Not fancy

Janet likes plain food rather than spicy food.

Plane (Noun) Shortened version of airplane

The plane departed for Florida early this morning.

Where (Adverb) in what position or circumstance

Where is the remote control?

Wear (Verb) Be dressed in

I decided to wear my green sweater today.

No	(Adverb) Express refusal	
	No! I will not let you copy my homework.	
Know	(Verb) Have knowledge	
	Christofer didn't know where he left his sneakers.	
Here	(Adverb) At this place	
	Is your homework here or at home?	
Hear	(Verb) Listen	
	Did you hear the new song by Beyonce?	

Let's Practice

Choose the correct word for each sentence. Then check your answers in the back of the book.

1. The brothers spent hours playing .... video games. (there / their / they're)

2. Molly ordered a .... donut rather than one with sprinkles. (plane / plain)

3. Jayme looked .... his binder for the homework. (threw / through)

4. I don't know .... I should go for a run or a hike. (whether / weather)

5. The .... of the fire was devastating. (effect / affect)

6. Melissa has .... many pairs of shoes. (to / too/ two)

7. My parents .... the decisions I make. (effect / affect)

8. The teacher asked Michele to read the paragraph ________________.
(allowed / aloud)

9. Listen closely, and you will ________________ the sounds of crickets.
(here / hear)

Although not a homophone, *than* and *then* are often confused. Read the notes below and then try one last question.

Then (Adverb) Next in order of time or place

We went to the movies, and then we ate pizza.

Than (Conjunction) Used in making a comparison

Jonathan is taller than I.

10. I like math better ________________ science.
(then / than)

Answers are on page 165.

Writing Interesting Dialogue

When people talk, it is called dialogue. Dialogue can make a story more exciting if it is done well, but it can be tricky. There are many rules for dialogue and hints to make it interesting. When writing dialogue, you are going to use quotation marks around words the character is speaking. You will also sometimes include a tag to tell the reader which character is talking.

Let's first look at punctuating dialogue. Review the rules of dialogue and read the examples. Then, you will have a chance to practice.

Punctuating Dialogue

When the tag is in front of the quotation…

- Use a comma before the quotation mark
- Capitalize the first word within the quotation marks
- Include end punctuation inside the quotation marks

For example:

Mr. Riccardi exclaimed, "Fifth graders are awesome!"

When the tag is behind the quotation...

- Capitalize the first letter of the quotation
- Use a comma, question mark, or exclamation point before the tag but inside the quotation marks
- Use a period at the end of the sentence

For example:

"What is the hypothesis?" asked Mrs. Magliato.

"Please take out your math homework," Ms. Blayne instructed.

"We won the game!" Coach Scire exclaimed.

When the tag interrupts the sentence:

- Capitalize the first letter of the sentence
- Use a comma inside the quotation before the tag and outside the quotation after the tag
- Do not capitalize the second half of the quote, unless it is a proper noun
- Include end punctuation inside the quotation marks

For example:

"This story," Ms. Perillo said, "is one of my favorites."

"We will board the bus at 9:15," Ms. Fava said, "and arrive at the museum around 10:00."

WARNING: These rules apply only if a sentence is interrupted. Make sure the sentences are not independent. Independent sentences will include end punctuation after the tag and begin with a capital letter.

For example:

"We will meet by the entrance at 3:00," Mr. DeMarco instructed. "Once everyone is present, we will walk back to the buses."

Let's Practice

Rewrite the following sentences using the rules of dialogue. Don't forget to check your capitalization. Then, check your answers in the back of the book.

1. who handed in their permission slips Mrs. Jones asked

2. nick said I'll be in my room if you need me

3. on Tuesday you can come bowling said Samantha if you like soccer, you should come to the park on Saturday

4. today we will practice passing and dribbling Coach Magnotti said

5. we will begin the experiment by gathering our materials Ms. Kaufhold directed and then we will dissect the worm

Answers are on page 166.

Writing good dialogue does not end at punctuation and capitalization. In order for dialogue to be effective, it needs to be surrounded by good narration. Narration is the story. Dialogue without narration is boring. Read the example below.

"What's wrong?" Robbie asked Mason.

"Nothing," Mason answered.

"I know something is bothering you," Robbie responded. "Just spill it."

"I'm failing math, and Mom and Dad are going to ground me," Mason replied.

"I can help you," Robbie said. "I'll tutor you after school."

Now, read the same dialogue with narration. Pay attention to how the writing has changed and improved because of the words surrounding the dialogue.

Mason sat on his bedroom floor with his head in his hands. The door creaked open and his older brother Robbie poked his head through the door. "What's wrong? Robbie asked.

"Nothing," Mason answered staring down at the floor, trying to hold in the tears.

"I know something is bothering you," Robbie responded as he sat next to his little brother. "Just spill it." Robbie lovingly put his arm around Mason, who was four years younger.

"I'm failing math, and Mom and Dad are going to ground me," Mason finally replied with a look of desperation.

"I can help you," Robbie said. "I'll tutor you after school." A look of relief came across Mason's face. Maybe Mom and Dad wouldn't be so mad if Robbie was going to help him.

With narration, the reader learns more about the characters and plot. This is more interesting dialogue than the previous passage.

Let's Practice

Read the boring dialogue. Then rewrite it with narration to make it more interesting for the reader.

"Come on Leo. No one's going to find out," Harley said.

"I don't know," Leo replied.

"I'm sure Ryan will let me copy. He's a good friend," Harley said.

"It's just that I studied really hard and I don't want to lose points if we get caught," Leo said.

"Trust me, we won't get caught," Harley replied.

"Maybe you should ask Ryan," Leo said.

Using I And Me

It is easy to confuse or misuse "I" and "me" when writing or speaking, but there is an easy fix to the problem. "I" is a pronoun and must be the subject of a sentence. "Me" is a pronoun that must be used as the object of a sentence. This means it will receive the action of the verb. Read the examples below.

I = pronoun used as a subject
I am going to the mall. Kelly and I are going to the mall.

Me = pronoun used as an object
Kelly is going to the mall with me. Kelly is going to the mall with Rachel and me.

It is often confusing whether to use "I" or "me" when writing a sentence with more than one subject or more than one object. There is an easy test to figure out the correct use. Simply remove the other noun from the sentence and decide if it makes sense. Look at the examples below.

John and me went to the dance on Friday.

Remove the other noun, John, and see if it makes sense.

Me went to the dance on Friday. (Does not make sense)

I went to the dance on Friday. (Makes sense)

Correct sentence: John and I went to the dance on Friday.

Based on the text, we can figure out the sentence should read, "John and I went to the dance." Furthermore, "I" is part of the subject; therefore, we know it is correct.

Let's look at one more example and then you will practice.

Sophie came with Jessie and I to the amusement park.

Remove the other noun, Jessie, and see if it makes sense.

Sophie came with I to the amusement park. (Does not make sense)

Sophie came with me to the amusement park. (Makes sense)

Correct sentence: Sophie came with Jessie and me to the amusement park.

In this sentence, the pronoun "me" is the object, not the subject, of the sentence. The subject of the sentence is Sophie.

Let's Practice

Complete each sentence with either "I" or "me," and then check your answers in the back of the book.

1. Mia, Hannah, Rhea, and ______________________ will be a group for the project.
2. Toby and ______________________ went to the library to study for the science exam.
3. Would you like to hang out with Sam, Nicole, and ______________________?
4. Please, come to the dance with Dan and ______________________.
5. Michele hit Grace and ______________________ home with her triple.

Answers are on page 166.

Answers to Practice Questions

Chapter 1

Interacting with Text (pages 9–10)

Possible answer: Although students are offered a complete lunch representing each food group, many toss away the healthy options. This is unhealthy for children.

Let's Practice (pages 11–12)

1. Cause and effect
2. Problem and solution
3. Sequential
4. Compare and contrast

Let's Practice (pages 12–14)

Paragraph 1

1. Possible Central Idea: As you decide the best pet for you and your family, you will need to weigh the positives and negatives of owning either a dog or a cat.
2. Compare and contrast because it shows the positives and negatives of owning a dog or cat.
3. Author is comparing pets and looking at the positives and negatives of each. Signal words: *yet* and *however*

Paragraph 2

1. Possible Central Idea: Teens should not smoke because it is dangerous.
2. Cause and effect because the passage shows what happens as a result of smoking.
3. Reed Johnson smoked. The effect is he is ill and out of work. His family has to struggle paying the bills. Reed started smoking as a teenager. The effect is he's ill as an adult. The article clearly shows the effects of smoking.

Let's Practice (pages 16–20)

1. Part A. **D** Law or rule

Part B. You should have underlined

Yet, there is still debate among students about whether these new laws are fair and parents about whether these rules work.

And

Students feel they are old enough to make their own food choices and don't agree with the government mandating the food they eat.

2. Part A. **D** problem and solution

   Part B. **A and E** *This is a growing problem across the country.* There are many possible solutions for improving school lunches.

3.

MAIN IDEAS	SUPPORTING DETAILS
Schools should be the only ones controlling school lunches and making rules abou the foods served.	Childhood obesity has more than doubled over the past three years.
It's time to examine cafeteria food regulations and find a way to increase the amounts of fruits and vegetables eaten.	**The school reports, "Students going to recess before lunch, eat more and waste less than kids going to recess after lunch."**
New cafeteria regulations are working just fine.	Many parents are unaware of the food being eaten by their children at school.
There should be no regulations because kids can make their own food choices.	When kids step into the cafeteria line they are offered a well-balanced meal.
Parents should be in control of what their kids eat.	**I eat more vegetables at home because we buy the things I like, and they taste better." This may be a simple solution, as long as the vegetables taste good.**

Practice Time! (pages 21–25)

1. Part A. **A** Deliberately, unfriendly behavior

   Part B. **D and F.** The study compared the number of hours spent playing violent video games to aggressive behaviors, which included hitting, kicking, and fighting other kids. Cameron, a fifth grader in South Bound Brook, claims that all of his friends play video games and it doesn't make them angry or aggressive.

2.

PROS	CONS
Boost brainpower	Kids mimic fighting behaviors
Movement and exercise opportunities	Leads to more aggressive behaviors
CONCLUSION	
Parents need to closely monitor video game use	

3. Part A. **B** The author provides statistical evidence.

   Part B. **C** *More than 85% of all parents do not actually monitor the rating of video games.*

4. Part A. **A** Kids who play video games learn how to think and do well in school.

   Part B. **D** *Video games actually boost brainpower.*

Chapter 2

Begin at the Beginning

Text 2 (pages 31–33)

1. Part A. **C** essential or much needed

   Part B. **A** *We must do everything possible to provide them the nutrition they need.*

2.

~~The new meal requirements will raise standards for the first time in more than fifteen years.~~	✘
Making sure that kids are offered both fruits and vegetables each day, more whole grains, and portion sizes and calorie counts designed to maintain a healthy weight.	3
"Improving the quality of the school meals is a critical step in building a healthy future for our kids," said Vilsack.	1
The final standards make the same kinds of practical changes that many parents are already encouraging at home.	2
~~As parents, we try to prepare decent meals, limit how much junk food our kids eat, and ensure they have a reasonably balanced diet.~~	✘

The regulations are for school lunches, so the most important details will be about school lunches. Keep your main idea in mind when answering a question like this on the PARCC.

3. Part A. ***C*** The author makes connections to what parents do at home.
   Part B. **B and D paragraphs 2 and 4.** In paragraph 2, the author discusses the foods parents serve at home and even quotes Michele Obama saying, "We want the food they get at school to be the same kind of food we would serve at our own kitchen tables." In paragraph 4, the author states, "The final standards make the same kinds of practical changes that many parents are already encouraging at home." In addition, the author provides a list of examples.

Text 3 (pages 34–35)

1.

OLD MENU	BOTH	NEW MENU
Juice	Low fat milk	Low fat cheese
More canned fruit	Whole grains	More fresh vegetables and fruits

2. Part A. **B** With the new, healthy changes, most meals will look very different in order to make them healthier.

   Part B. **B and C** Tuesday and Wednesday. Friday shows a healthier version of pizza, which is similar rather than different. Since this is a similar choice it also eliminates **A** as a correct answer.

Let's Practice (pages 52-53)

1. **C and E**
2. **A and C**
3. **A and E**

Let's Practice (page 55)

1. Subject and Predicate.
2. **A and C**
3. **A and C**

Practice Time!

An excerpt from *Tim Tebow: A Promise Kept* by Mike Klis (2012) (pages 57-59)

1. Part A. **D** causing people to separate into two opposite groups

   Part B. You should have underlined *This means most fans either really like or really dislike him.*

2. Part A. **B** It is difficult to understand why people do not like Tebow.

Part B. **C and D** Tebow never says a bad word about anybody. He was 4–1 as a starter for a team that was 1–4 before he took control.

3. Part A. **D** He respects Tim Tebow.

   Part B. You should have underlined *Most of all, Tebow is a winner. No matter how poorly a game is going, he never quits and often figures out how to win at the end.*

***What Makes Them Beautiful* (pages 60-62)**

1. Part A. **C** Come together for a common purpose

   Part B. **A** *Assured him that they and the fans still adored him*

2. Part A. **C** The boys were popular, but people were rooting for them like they weren't so popular.

   Part B. **D** *They looked and behaved more like pop stars but were still recognizable as the boys who had appeared for their first auditions.*

3.

TIM TEBOW	BOTH	HARRY FROM ONE DIRECTION
Being kind and staying positive are more powerful than negativity.	Always do your best, regardless of what people say.	Everyone gets nervous.
It takes courage to overcome put downs from others.	At times, everyone needs to rely on personal strength to overcome the tough times	Friends help get you through tough times.

Excerpt from *Justin Bieber Confidential* by Robert Scott (2014) (pages 63–64)

1. Part A. **B** depicts or shows

   Part B. **A** *There are songs that teens can relate to, as far as parents not being together and divorce and just stuff that happens in everyday life.*

2. Part A. ***C*** Justin is grateful to his fans because they are critical to his success.

   Part B. **A** *Thanks to you, my family is having a chance at a better life.*

Sample Research Task (pages 65–70)

Have you ever been laughed at? Told you couldn't do something? Criticized about your performance? At some point in our lives, most of us have had to deal with people being insensitive or mean. Some people turn around and treat the aggressor in the same way, while others take the high road and ignore it. All three of the celebrities in the articles had to deal with negativity in some way, but each was able to overcome it and have a positive outlook on life.

According to the article, Tim Tebow is the most "polarizing" player in football. This means people either love him or hate him. This must be extremely challenging for a public figure to constantly hear and see mean, negative comments about themselves. Yet, no matter what people say, "Tebow never says a bad word about anybody." Even when these negative words came from other football players or announcers, Tebow stayed positive and played well. Despite the criticism, Tebow was able to take the Broncos to the playoffs that year. Tim Tebow is truly a strong person.

Likewise Harry Styles from One Direction also had to overcome negativity from the public. After one of his first live appearances, where his nerves showed on stage, he was "devastated by the extent of the abuse that he found" on social media sites. Unlike Tebow, Harry leaned on his friends, bandmates, and fans to give him encouragement. Nonetheless, Harry needed to be strong and overcome the criticism.

Justin Bieber also had to overcome a negative situation. However, for him, it began early in his life. In the article, Justin says, "My message is: you can do anything if you put your mind to it. I grew up below the poverty line; I didn't have as much as other people did." Yet, he found great success. As a result, he showed an immense appreciation for his fans, especially at the beginning of his career. According to Justin Bieber Confidential (2014), he was quoted as saying, "I just wanted to add a note thanking you personally for all the support. You are helping a kid from a small town chase a dream, and I am forever grateful. Thanks to you, my family is having a chance at a better life, and I am getting to go and see places I could have never dreamed of." With hard work, Justin was able to overcome a negative situation and make a better life for himself and his family.

In conclusion, each of these young men demonstrated a special ability to be strong and ignore the negative comments or situations faced in life. Each of them made their lives better through their personal attitude and choices. So the next time someone laughs at you, criticizes you, or says you can't do something, take a tip from any of these three guys and turn the situation around. Prove that you can do anything, if you put your mind to it.

Chapter 3

Let's Practice (page 76)

1. Clues: A lion pounces. I think a lion pounces to catch or attack other animals for food. Mom is going to pounce because she is angry.

   Definition: Pounce sounds like it would be a sudden attack.

2. Clues: The paper was jabbing back and forth, so it sounds like it is moving in some way. Mom looked like a knight trying to slay the evil dragon. A knight would use a sword to do this and would wave it around.

   Definition: Jabbed must mean that mom quickly stabbed or thrust the paper forward toward Connor like a knife or sword.

The Plot of "The Look" (pages 80–81)

1. *Exposition*. What background information do we know?
   - Connor is coming home from elementary school.
   - He lives with his mom.
2. *Rising Actions*. What events and complications happen in the story?
   - Mom confronts Connor about the letter from school.
   - Connor had already erased phone messages from the teacher and principal.
   - Then, he lies about shooting spitballs and blames his best friend Robbie.
   - Connor's mom calls Robbie's mom to straighten things out.
3. *Climax or Turning Point*. What part of the story does Connor make a decision that will change the course of the story?

   Connor interrupts his mom's phone call to admit the truth.
4. *Falling Action*. What happens after the climax that will lead to the resolution?

   Connor realizes his mom wasn't really talking to Robbie's mom. He is sent to his room.
5. *Resolution*. What will happen at the end of the story?

   Connor will be punished and he thinks it will be a biggie.

The Theme of "The Look" (page 82)

Possible answers:

✔ Honesty is the best policy.
✔ Treat others the way you want to be treated.
✔ Don't lie to your mom.

Let's Practice (pages 85–88)

1. **Part A. D** Outcome or result of something that happened earlier

   Part B. C *I knew I deserved whatever punishment she gave me.*
2. **Part A. B** metaphor. The sentence describes Mom and a lioness ready to pounce without using like or as.

   Part B. A Mom is angry and ready to grill him as soon as he enters the house.
3. **Part A. B** The turning point. This is the turning point because it is at this moment when an event changes the story and the character begins heading toward a resolution of the story. When Connor finally admits he was wrong, the falling action begins.

   Part B. You should have underlined *I couldn't take it any longer.*

4. Part A. **B** Do not lie because it will get you in trouble.

   Part B. **D** paragraph 8. In this paragraph, Connor realizes he was tricked and he will be getting punished for lying to his mom.

Practice Time!

"A Night to Remember" (pages 94-98)

1. Part A. ***A*** with great attention.

   Part B. You should have underlined *She turned her head to the right and listened intently. Then, she turned her head to the left and did the same thing. Her ears only found silence, but then she heard leaves rustling from behind.*

2. Part A. ***A*** still.

   Part B. **D** Abby froze, her eyes wide.

3. Part A. **B** It represents the turning point.

   Part B. **D** *Someone was coming to save her.* At this point, the falling action begins.

4. Part A. ***A*** They show that Abby is not happy about the hard work necessary for camping.

   Part B. **D** *"This is hard work," she complained to her best friend Jenna. "I shouldn't be sweating."*

"The Ant and the Grasshopper" (pages 99-101)

1. Part A. **B** hard work

   Part B. ***C*** *"I am helping to lay up food for the winter," said the Ant, "and recommend you to do the same."*

2. Part A. ***C*** Hard work pays off.

   Part B. **D** *When the winter came the Grasshopper had no food and found itself dying of hunger, while it saw the ants distributing every day corn and grain from the stores they had collected in the summer.*

3.

~~The ant carried an ear of corn.~~	✘
Grasshopper tries to get Ant to stop working and talk to him, but Ant keeps working.	1
When winter comes, Grasshopper doesn't have enough food but the ants do.	3
Ant advises Grasshopper to work hard to collect food, but Grasshopper doesn't listen.	2
~~Grasshopper was hopping and singing across the field.~~	✘

Prose Constructed Response (pages 101–106)

Possible response:

Did you ever want something really bad? What did you do in order to get it? Did you have to work hard? Save money? Put in extra time? Or did you complain and walk away? Most people learn early that things don't come easy. You have to work for what you want. In "A Night to Remember" and "The Ant and the Grasshopper" neither main character wants to put the time or energy into working hard, and in both situations, they paid for it in the end.

Abby, the main character in "A Night to Remember" went on a camping trip with her Girl Scout troop and expected to be treated like she was at a resort. She complained to her friend Jenna, "I shouldn't be sweating. This is supposed to be a vacation, right?" In order to have a good camping trip, you need to set up camp, gather firewood, and cook food. It's work but also fun for most people. In this case, Abby didn't want to do her part. When everyone was collecting firewood, she detoured, looking for a "place to plop down and relax in the sun." As a result of not listening and taking the easy way out, Abby was lost in the woods. This could have been a disaster for her. She could have gone hungry or been hurt. Luckily, her friends and troop leader found her.

Likewise, Grasshopper, from "The Ant and the Grasshopper" didn't want to gather food for the winter. While the ant was working hard, Grasshopper was hopping and playing around. Even when Ant suggested he gather food, Grasshopper refused to listen. He responded, "We have got plenty of food at present." Unfortunately, Grasshopper also paid the price for his laziness. When winter came, the ants had food to eat but Grasshopper had nothing. In the end, he learned his lesson to be better prepared.

Both stories had good examples of the importance of working hard and doing what you are supposed to do. Both Abby and Grasshopper put their lives at risk. Hopefully, they learned a lesson and will change in the future. The next time you want something, keep Abby and Grasshopper in mind. Put the time in and don't be lazy because you might be putting yourself in a dangerous situation.

Chapter 4

Practice Time!

Sample Story 1 (pages 120–125)

It was summer once again. Grasshopper woke up early and looked out at the morning sunrise. It had been a long winter, but he survived. I knew I could do it, he thought to himself and I only needed a teeny, tiny, little bit of help from the ants. They had warned him that winter would be hard if he didn't store food, but when it came down to it, they bailed him out with the scraps that none of the other ants wanted or needed. Grasshopper would not have survived without their generosity.

Now, it was a new year and Grasshopper was ready. When the time comes, I'll gather food this year, he thought determinedly.

Yet, when he glanced across the meadow, he just wanted to happily hop through the field. As he debated what to do, he heard a small voice behind him. "Are you ready to collect, Grasshopper?" Ant asked in a meek voice.

"Just a quick jaunt through the meadow and I'll be ready to start," Grasshopper replied as he quickly took off hopping as hard as his Grasshopper legs would carry him. When he made it to the center of the field, he thought, what am I doing? I need to collect food or I'll spend the winter hungry again. He turned around but Ant was nowhere to be found.

Grasshopper started to gather food alone. It was hard work and soon Grasshopper was dirty and exhausted. He looked at the small pile he had built up for himself. Just then the wind began to blow. He ran over to his supply and tried to shield his treasure. However, it was not his day and he watched the pile disappear to nothing.

As Grasshopper headed home, Ant ran up to him excitedly. "You are not going to believe this," he shouted. "I spent the morning gathering a little food but then I stopped for a lunch. When I finished eating, my pile was triple the size."

Grasshopper gasped. "You have my food," he shouted.

"No way," Ant replied as he stomped back to his house.

The next day Grasshopper woke up bright and early, determined to gather twice the amount of food as yesterday. This time he got right to work without any playtime. Again, he gathered a nice size pile when he spotted a great spot over the hill for gathering. Just a quick run and then pile will be complete. But when Grasshopper returned, his food was gone. "Where did my food go?" Grasshopper shouted as he stomped his feet.

That night, Grasshopper decided he needed a new plan. He woke up bright and early the next morning, but this time he didn't head to the meadow, he headed to Ant's house. When Ant came outside, Grasshopper quickly asked, "Will you help me gather food today?"

"I thought you'd never ask," Ant replied with a smile.

Sample Story 2 (pages 126–130)

Ugh, Bryce groaned. Today was the day. Today, Bryce would need to face a new school in a new town. "I don't want to go," he complained as he pulled the covers over his head. "Everyone else will know each other and I'll be the weird new kid."

"It will be fun," his mom said with a cheery smile pasted on her face.

"I don't believe you," he mumbled as he rolled onto his other side.

After another fifteen minutes of arguing, Bryce finally pulled himself out of bed and began to get ready for school. He pulled a t-shirt and jeans out of his dresser, brushed his teeth, and headed downstairs for breakfast. Finally, it was time to wait for the bus.

The bus will probably forget me, he thought as he shuffled down to the corner. However, when he got there he saw two other boys waiting. They quickly started talking about the football games from the day before. Bryce couldn't resist. Football was his favorite sport. When the bus arrived, the boys headed to the back of the bus, but Bryce stopped and sat in the middle. I'm sure they don't want me to sit with them he thought to himself. He turned and stared out the window, dreading the rest of the day.

As he walked into school, the bell rang and he slowly walked to his homeroom. He sat down in a seat, wondering if he was stealing someone else's chair. Oh well, he thought to himself. Unexpectedly, his homeroom teacher Mr. Grover greeted him with a high five and then introduced Bryce to the class. As the other kids smiled at him, Bryce felt a small twitch of a smile on his own face, but that wasn't going to make the day any better.

When the bell rang, Bryce realized he made it through the day. His backpack was jammed with pages of homework he needed to do in order to catch up with the class. I'll never get this done, he thought to himself. Could the day get any worse? He sat alone at lunch, barely talked to anyone in class, yet everyone kept smiling at him and saying hello.

When he got onto the bus, Bryce heard two voices yell out to him. "Hey, come sit with us." It was the boys from the morning. "I'm Jake and this is Angelo," Jake said. After introductions, they continued the discussion about the best play of each Sunday football game and made predictions for the following weekend. As they stepped off the bus, Jake asked, "Do you want to come over and we'll help you catch up on your work? I know what it's like being the new guy."

"That would be awesome," he replied with a smile. Maybe this wouldn't be so bad after all.

Chapter 5

Let's Practice (pages 132–133)

1. The lonely boy. These words form only a subject. The sentence is about a lonely boy, but what did the lonely boy do? You need to provide the answer by writing a predicate or action for the sentence.

   Possible answers:

   The lonely boy tried to make new friends.

   The lonely boy joined the basketball team.

   The lonely boy missed his best friend.

2. The angry teacher. This sentence consists of only a subject. Who is the sentence about? We know it is about the angry teacher, but what did the angry teacher do? You need to provide the action or predicate for the sentence.

Possible answers:

The angry teacher gave the students detention.

The angry teacher yelled at the class.

The angry teacher stomped her foot.

3. Played video games for hours. This sentence has the action but doesn't tell the reader who is doing the action. Who is playing video games for hours? You need to provide the answer by writing the subject.

   Possible answers:

   Jordan and Paul played video games for hours.

   The competitive sisters played video games for hours.

4. Announced he won the lottery. This sentence includes only the action but not the subject. Who is announcing he won the lottery.

   Possible answers:

   My cousin announced he won the lottery.

   Mr. Turner, my neighbor, announced he won the lottery.

Let's Practice (page 135)

1. Tyler dove for the ball, he made the third out.

   Tyler dove for the ball, and he made the third out.

   Tyler dove for the ball. He made the third out.

   Since Tyler dove for the ball, he made the third out.

2. Grace performed in the talent show she won first place.

   Grace performed in the talent show. She won first place.

   Grace performed in the talent show, and she won first place.

   When Grace performed in the talent show, she won first place.

3. My cat cuddled on the couch, he purred when I pet him.

   My cat cuddled on the couch, and he purred when I pet him.

   My cat cuddled on the couch. He purred when I pet him.

   Cuddling on the couch, my cat purred when I pet him.

4. Reed studied for her science test she aced it.

   Reed studied for her science test. She aced it.

   Reed studied for her science test, and she aced it.

   When Reed studied for her science test, she aced it.

Let's Practice (page 136)

1. Simple Sentence. A simple sentence needs to include a subject and predicate.

   Possible answers:

   I love to read thriller books.

   I play soccer in the fall.

2. Compound Sentence. Each compound sentence consists of two independent clauses. Both could stand alone as a complete sentence.

   Possible answers:

   I love to read thriller books, and then I write thriller stories.

   I play soccer in the fall, and I play baseball in the spring.

3. Complex Sentence. Writing an independent clause with one or more dependent clauses forms a complex sentence.

   Possible answers:

   I love to read thriller books and write them as well.

   After playing baseball in the spring, I play soccer in the fall.

Let's Practice (page 137)

1. In order to earn my allowance, I need to clean my room, walk the dog, and empty the dishwasher.
2. Elizabeth, do you like to listen to music after school?
3. Yes, I do like to listen to music in my free time.

Let's Practice (pages 140–141)

1. The brothers spent hours playing their video games.
2. Molly ordered a plain donut rather than one with sprinkles.
3. Jayme looked through his binder for the homework.
4. I don't know whether I should go for a run or a hike.
5. The effect of the fire was devastating.
6. Melissa has too many pairs of shoes.
7. My parents affect the decisions I make.
8. The teacher asked Michele to read the paragraph aloud.
9. Listen closely, and you will hear the sounds of crickets.
10. I like math better than science.

Let's Practice (page 143)

1. "Who handed in their permission slips?" Mrs. Jones asked.
2. Nick said, "I'll be in my room if you need me."
3. "On Tuesday you can come bowling," said Samantha. "If you like soccer, you should come to the park on Saturday."
4. "Today we will practice passing and dribbling," Coach Magnotti said.
5. "We will begin the experiment by gathering our materials," Ms. Kaufhold directed, "and then we will dissect the worm."

Let's Practice (page 147)

1. Mia, Hannah, Rhea, and I will be a group for the project.
2. Toby and I went to the library to study for the science exam.
3. Would you like to hang out with Sam, Nicole, and me?
4. Please, come to the dance with Dan and me.
5. Michele hit Grace and me home with her triple.

Practice Tests

Congratulations! You have completed the practice chapters to prepare for the PARCC. Now you will have the opportunity to put all of this knowledge to use as you take two practice tests for the language arts portion of the test. The first test will be the Performance-Based Assessment (PBA), which includes a literature task, a research task, and a narrative task. All three will have a written component. The second test is a practice End-of-Year Assessment (EOY), which includes literature and informational tasks. Neither section will include a written response. Make sure you read the directions on each section and pay close attention to what the task is asking you to complete. Good luck! When you are finished, check your answers in the back of the book.

PRACTICE TEST 1
Performance-Based Assessment (PBA)

Part 1: Literary Analysis Task

Directions: Read the following selection from *Black Beauty* and answer the questions that follow. You will have about 80 minutes to complete this task. You may use additional time if needed.

"My Breaking In"
Excerpt from *Black Beauty* by Anna Sewell

1 I was now beginning to grow handsome; my coat had grown fine and soft, and was bright black. I had one white foot and a pretty white star on my forehead. I was thought very handsome; my master would not sell me till I was four years old; he said lads ought not to work like men, and colts ought not to work like horses till they were quite grown up.

2 When I was four years old Squire Gordon came to look at me. He examined my eyes, my mouth, and my legs; he felt them all down; and then I had to walk and trot and gallop before him. He seemed to like me, and said, "When he has been well broken in he will do very well." My master said he would break me in himself, as he should not like me to be frightened or hurt, and he lost no time about it, for the next day he began.

3 Every one may not know what breaking in is, therefore I will describe it. It means to teach a horse to wear a saddle and bridle, and to carry on his back a man, woman or child; to go just the way they wish, and to go quietly. Besides this he has to learn to wear a collar, a crupper, and a breeching, and to stand still while they are put on; then to have a cart or a chaise fixed behind, so that he cannot walk or trot without dragging it after him; and he must go fast or slow, just as his driver wishes. He must never start at what he sees, nor speak to other horses, nor bite, nor kick, nor have any will of his own; but always do his master's will, even though he may be very tired or hungry; but the worst of all is, when his harness is once on, he may neither jump for joy nor lie down for weariness. So you see this breaking in is a great thing.

4 I had of course long been used to a halter and a headstall, and to be led about in the fields and lanes quietly, but now I was to have a bit and bridle; my master gave me some oats as usual, and after a good deal of coaxing he got the bit into my mouth, and the bridle fixed, but it was a nasty thing! Those who have never had a bit in their mouths cannot think how bad it feels; a great piece of cold hard steel as thick as a man's finger to be pushed into one's mouth, between one's teeth, and over one's tongue, with the ends coming out at the corner of your mouth, and held fast there by straps over your head, under your throat, round your nose, and under your chin; so that no way in the world can you get rid of the nasty hard thing; it is very bad! Yes, very bad! At least I thought so; but I knew my mother always wore one when she went out, and all horses did when they were grown up; and so, what with the nice oats, and what with my master's pats, kind words, and gentle ways, I got to wear my bit and bridle.

5 Next came the saddle, but that was not half so bad; my master put it on my back very gently, while old Daniel held my head; he then made the girths fast under my body, patting and talking to me all the time; then I had a few oats, then a little leading about; and this he did every day till I began to look for the oats and the saddle. At length, one morning, my master got on my back and rode me round the meadow on the soft grass. It certainly did feel queer; but I must say I felt rather proud to carry my master, and as he continued to ride me a little every day I soon became accustomed to it.

6 The next unpleasant business was putting on the iron shoes; that too was very hard at first. My master went with me to the smith's forge, to see that I was not hurt or got any fright. The blacksmith took my feet in his hand, one after the other, and cut away some of the hoof.

It did not pain me, so I stood still on three legs till he had done them all. Then he took a piece of iron the shape of my foot, and clapped it on, and drove some nails through the shoe quite into my hoof, so that the shoe was firmly on. My feet felt very stiff and heavy, but in time I got used to it.

1. **Part A.** In paragraph 4, the narrator says, "My master gave me some oats as usual, and after a good deal of <u>coaxing</u> he got the bit into my mouth, and the bridle fixed, but it was a nasty thing!" Define <u>coaxing</u>.

   ○ A. To persuade

   ○ B. To feed

   ○ C. To brush

   ○ D. To anger

   Part B. Underline the sentence from paragraph 4 that best supports your answer to Part A.

   I had of course long been used to a halter and a headstall, and to be led about in the fields and lanes quietly, but now I was to have a bit and bridle; my master gave me some oats as usual, and after a good deal of <u>coaxing</u> he got the bit into my mouth, and the bridle fixed, but it was a nasty thing! Those who have never had a bit in their mouths cannot think how bad it feels; a great piece of cold hard steel as thick as a man's finger to be pushed into one's mouth, between one's teeth, and over one's tongue, with the ends coming out at the corner of your mouth, and held fast there by straps over your head, under your throat, round your nose, and under your chin; so that no way in the world can you get rid of the nasty hard thing; it is very bad! Yes, very bad! At least I thought so; but I knew my mother always wore one when she went out, and all horses did when they were grown up; and so, what with the nice oats, and what with my master's pats, kind words, and gentle ways, I got to wear my bit and bridle.

2. **Part A.** The narrator of the story is __________.

○ A. the master

○ B. a young girl

○ C. a young boy

○ D. a horse

Part B. Which two details from the text support the answer to Part A?

☐ A. *At length, one morning, my master got on my back and rode me round the meadow on the soft grass.*

☐ B. *The next unpleasant business was putting on the iron shoes; that too was very hard at first.*

☐ C. *When I was four years old Squire Gordon came to look at me.*

☐ D. *My feet felt very stiff and heavy, but in time I got used to it.*

3. **Part A.** How does the master feel about Black Beauty?

○ A. He does not care for Black Beauty.

○ B. He hopes to sell Black Beauty.

○ C. He loves Black Beauty.

○ D. He does not need Black Beauty.

Part B. How does the reader know the master truly cares for Black Beauty?

○ A. The master said he would break Black Beauty in himself, as he should not like him to be frightened or hurt.

○ B. The master went with Black Beauty to the blacksmith for shoes.

○ C. The master bought new clothes for Black Beauty.

○ D. Both A and B

4. **Part A.** How are Black Beauty's shoes different from the shoes you wear today?

○ A. They are iron and held on with nails.

○ B. They are silver and held on with nails.

○ C. They are leather like shoes today.

○ D. They are black and shiny.

Part B. What would be the closest type of shoes to Black Beauty's that you would wear?

- ○ A. Sandals
- ○ B. Roller skates
- ○ C. Slippers
- ○ D. Socks

5. **Part A.** What will happen to Black Beauty after he is broken in?

- ○ A. He will run a race.
- ○ B. He will see his mother.
- ○ C. He will eat oats.
- ○ D. He will go live with Squire Gordon.

Part B. What evidence from the text provides proof of your answer to Part A? Write the answer below.

----

6. **Part A.** How did Black Beauty feel when he carried his master?

- ○ A. Tired
- ○ B. Proud
- ○ C. Angry
- ○ D. All of the above

Part B. What paragraph helped you decide your answer for Part A?

- ○ A. Paragraph 1
- ○ B. Paragraph 5
- ○ C. Paragraph 6
- ○ D. Paragraph 2

Directions: Read the story of Mary and then answer the questions that follow.

"Mistress Mary, Quite Contrary"

From *The Secret Garden* by Frances Hodgson Burnett

1 Mary had liked to look at her mother from a distance and she had thought her very pretty, but as she knew very little of her she could scarcely have been expected to love her or to miss her very much when she was gone. She did not miss her at all, in fact, and as she was a self-absorbed child she gave her entire thought to herself, as she had always done. If she had been older she would no doubt have been very anxious at being left alone in the world, but she was very young, and as she had always been taken care of, she supposed she always would be. What she thought was that she would like to know if she was going to nice people, who would be polite to her and give her her own way as her Ayah and the other native servants had done.

2 She knew that she was not going to stay at the English clergyman's house where she was taken at first. She did not want to stay. The English clergyman was poor and he had five children nearly all the same age and they wore shabby clothes and were always quarreling and snatching toys from each other. Mary hated their untidy bungalow and was so disagreeable to them that after the first day or two nobody would play with her. By the second day they had given her a nickname which made her furious.

3 It was Basil who thought of it first. Basil was a little boy with impudent blue eyes and a turned-up nose, and Mary hated him. She was playing by herself under a tree, just as she had been playing the day the cholera broke out. She was making heaps of earth and paths for a garden and Basil came and stood near to watch her. Presently he got rather interested and suddenly made a suggestion.

4 "Why don't you put a heap of stones there and pretend it is a rockery?" he said. "There in the middle," and he leaned over her to point.

5 "Go away!" cried Mary. "I don't want boys. Go away!"

6 For a moment Basil looked angry, and then he began to tease. He was always teasing his sisters. He danced round and round her and made faces and sang and laughed.

7 "Mistress Mary, quite contrary,

How does your garden grow?

With silver bells, and cockle shells,

And marigolds all in a row."

8 He sang it until the other children heard and laughed, too; and the crosser Mary got, the more they sang "Mistress Mary, quite contrary"; and after that as long as she stayed with them they called her "Mistress Mary Quite Contrary" when they spoke of her to each other, and often when they spoke to her.

9 "You are going to be sent home," Basil said to her, "at the end of the week. And we're glad of it."

10 "I am glad of it, too," answered Mary. "Where is home?"

11 "She doesn't know where home is!" said Basil, with seven-year-old scorn. "It's England, of course. Our grandmama lives there and our sister Mabel was sent to her last year. You are not going to your grandmama. You have none. You are going to your uncle. His name is Mr. Archibald Craven."

12 "I don't know anything about him," snapped Mary.

13 "I know you don't," Basil answered. "You don't know anything. Girls never do. I heard father and mother talking about him. He lives in a great, big, <u>desolate</u> old house in the country and no one goes near him. He's so cross he won't let them, and they wouldn't come if he would let them. He's a hunchback, and he's horrid."

14 "I don't believe you," said Mary; and she turned her back and stuck her fingers in her ears, because she would not listen any more. But she thought over it a great deal afterward; and

when Mrs. Crawford told her that night that she was going to sail away to England in a few days and go to her uncle, Mr. Archibald Craven, who lived at Misselthwaite Manor, she looked so stony and stubbornly uninterested that they did not know what to think about her. They tried to be kind to her, but she only turned her face away when Mrs. Crawford attempted to kiss her, and held herself stiffly when Mr. Crawford patted her shoulder.

15 "She is such a plain child," Mrs. Crawford said pityingly, afterward. "And her mother was such a pretty creature. She had a very pretty manner, too, and Mary has the most unattractive ways I ever saw in a child. The children call her `Mistress Mary Quite Contrary,' and though it's naughty of them, one can't help understanding it."

1. **Part A.** What happened to Mary's mother?

- ○ A. She is on vacation.
- ○ B. She is working.
- ○ C. She died.
- ○ D. None of the above

Part B. Underline the sentence from paragraph 1 that best supports your answer to Part A.

Mary had liked to look at her mother from a distance and she had thought her very pretty, but as she knew very little of her she could scarcely have been expected to love her or to miss her very much when she was gone. She did not miss her at all, in fact, and as she was a self-absorbed child she gave her entire thought to herself, as she had always done. If she had been older she would no doubt have been very anxious at being left alone in the world, but she was very young, and as she had always been taken care of, she supposed she always would be. What she thought was that she would like to know if she was going to nice people, who would be polite to her and give her her own way as her Ayah and the other native servants had done.

2. Part A. In paragraph 1, Mary is described as self-absorbed. This means she ________________ .

- ○ A. is selfish
- ○ B. makes friends easily
- ○ C. is unhappy
- ○ D. Both A and B

Part B. Which phrase gives you a clue to the answer to Part A?

- ○ A. *she gave her entire thought to herself*
- ○ B. *she knew very little*
- ○ C. *If she had been older*
- ○ D. *she had thought her very pretty*

3. Part A. What nickname did the kids give Mary?

- ○ A. Mary had a little lamb
- ○ B. Mistress Mary quite contrary
- ○ C. Mean Mistress Mary
- ○ D. Mistress Mary always scary

Part B. What type of writing does her nickname come from?

- ○ A. Folktale
- ○ B. Nursery rhyme
- ○ C. Myth
- ○ D. Limerick

4. Part A. Archibald Craven's house is described as a great, big, desolate old house in the country. What does desolate mean?

- ○ A. Lovely
- ○ B. Scary
- ○ C. Huge
- ○ D. Dreary

Part B. What would best be described as desolate?

- ○ A. An abandoned amusement park
- ○ B. A dead end street
- ○ C. The beach in summertime
- ○ D. A school hallway

5. **Part A.** Basil described Archibald Craven as all of the following except.

- ○ A. cross
- ○ B. hunchback
- ○ C. horrid
- ○ D. greedy

Part B. Which of the choices in Part A refers to a physical condition? Write the answer below.

----

6. **Part A.** What is Mrs. Crawford's opinion of Mary?

- ○ A. She thinks Mary is like her mother.
- ○ B. She loves Mary like a daughter.
- ○ C. She is not fond of Mary.
- ○ D. She thinks Mary is a funny child.

Part B. Write the quote from Mrs. Crawford that tells you how she feels about Mary.

Writing Task

In the two readings completed so far, there are two different types of narrators. One narrator is an animal, and the other is telling the story of Mary. Write an essay describing how the narrator in a story can change the way you understand the story. Use specific examples from each text to support your answer.

Part 2: Research Task

Directions: Read each article about the Mars Curiosity Rover and answer the questions that follow. You will have about 80 minutes to complete this task. You may use additional time if needed.

Text 1

NASA's Mars Curiosity Rover Arrives at Martian Mountain

1 NASA's Mars Curiosity rover has reached the Red Planet's Mount Sharp, a Mount-Rainier-size mountain at the center of the vast Gale Crater and the rover mission's long-term prime destination.

2 "Curiosity now will begin a new chapter from an already outstanding introduction to the world," said Jim Green, director of NASA's Planetary Science Division at NASA Headquarters in Washington. "After a historic and innovative landing along with its successful science discoveries, the scientific sequel is upon us."

3 Curiosity's trek up the mountain will begin with an examination of the mountain's lower slopes. The rover is starting this process at an entry point near an outcrop called Pahrump Hills, rather than continuing on to the previously-planned, further entry point known as Murray Buttes. Both entry points lay along a boundary where the southern base layer of the mountain meets crater-floor deposits washed down from the crater's northern rim.

4 "It has been a long but historic journey to this Martian mountain," said Curiosity Project Scientist John Grotzinger of the California Institute of Technology in Pasadena. "The nature of the terrain at Pahrump Hills and just beyond it is a better place than Murray Buttes to learn about the significance of this contact. The exposures at the contact are better due to greater topographic relief."

5 The decision to head uphill sooner, instead of continuing to Murray Buttes, also draws from improved understanding of the region's geography provided by the rover's examinations of several outcrops during the past year. Curiosity currently is positioned at

the base of the mountain along a pale, distinctive geological feature called the Murray formation. Compared to neighboring crater-floor terrain, the rock of the Murray formation is softer and does not preserve impact scars, as well. As viewed from orbit, it is not as well-layered as other units at the base of Mount Sharp.

6 Curiosity made its first close-up study last month of two Murray formation outcrops, both revealing notable differences from the terrain explored by Curiosity during the past year. The first outcrop, called Bonanza King, proved too unstable for drilling, but was examined by the rover's instruments and determined to have high silicon content. A second outcrop, examined with the rover's telephoto Mast Camera, revealed a fine-grained, platy surface laced with sulfate-filled veins.

7 While some of these terrain differences are not apparent in observations made by NASA's Mars orbiters, the rover team still relies heavily on images taken by the agency's Mars Reconnaissance Orbiter (MRO) to plan Curiosity's travel routes and locations for study.

8 For example, MRO images helped the rover team locate mesas that are over 60 feet (18 meters) tall in an area of terrain shortly beyond Pahrump Hills, which reveal an exposure of the Murray formation uphill and toward the south. The team plans to use Curiosity's drill to acquire a sample from this site for analysis by instruments inside the rover. The site lies at the southern end of a valley Curiosity will enter this week from the north.

9 Though this valley has a sandy floor the length of two football fields, the team expects it will be an easier trek than the sandy-floored Hidden Valley, where last month Curiosity's wheels slipped too much for safe crossing.

10 Curiosity reached its current location after its route was modified earlier this year in response to excessive wheel wear. In late 2013, the team realized a region of Martian terrain littered with sharp, embedded rocks was poking holes in four of the rover's six wheels. This damage accelerated the rate of wear and tear beyond that for which the rover team had planned. In response, the team altered the rover's route to a milder terrain, bringing the rover farther south, toward the base of Mount Sharp.

11 "The wheels issue contributed to taking the rover farther south sooner than planned, but it is not a factor in the science-driven decision to start ascending here rather than continuing to Murray Buttes first," said Jennifer Trosper, Curiosity Deputy Project Manager at NASA's Jet Propulsion Laboratory in Pasadena, California. "We have been driving hard for many months to reach the entry point to Mount Sharp," Trosper said. "Now that we've made it, we'll be adjusting the operations style from a priority on driving to a priority on conducting the investigations needed at each layer of the mountain."

12 After landing inside Gale Crater in August 2012, Curiosity fulfilled in its first year of operations its major science goal of determining whether Mars ever offered environmental conditions favorable for microbial life. Clay-bearing sedimentary rocks on the crater floor, in an area called Yellowknife Bay, yielded evidence of a lakebed environment billions of years ago that offered fresh water, all of the key elemental ingredients for life, and a chemical source of energy for microbes.

13 NASA's Mars Science Laboratory Project continues to use Curiosity to assess ancient habitable environments and major changes in Martian environmental conditions. The destinations on Mount Sharp offer a series of geological layers that recorded different chapters in the environmental evolution of Mars.

14 The Mars Exploration Rover Project is one element of NASA's ongoing preparation for a human mission to the Red Planet in the 2030s. JPL built Curiosity and manages the project and MRO for NASA's Science Mission Directorate in Washington.

http://www.jpl.nasa.gov/m/news/news.php?release=2014-307 - .VBdYUUvQC-V

1. How do using words like "terrain," "lakebed," and "crater" help us understand what the Mars Rover sees?

   O A. It is similar to the ground on Earth.

   O B. They are words that describe the rover.

   O C. It helps the reader visualize what the ground is like.

   O D. Both A and C

2. What are the options for the scientists when the rover has mechanical problems like tire damage?

   O A. Send out an astronaut to make repairs.

   O B. Allow the robot to change its own tires.

   O C. Move the robot to a safer area.

   O D. Return the rover to its base.

3. Which sentence from the article tells the reader what NASA's goal is for the Rover?

   O A. *The Mars Exploration Rover Project is one element of NASA's ongoing preparation for a human mission to the Red Planet in the 2030s.*

   O B. *After landing inside Gale Crater in August 2012, Curiosity fulfilled in its first year of operations its major science goal of determining whether Mars ever offered environmental conditions favorable for microbial life.*

   O C. *Curiosity currently is positioned at the base of the mountain along a pale, distinctive geological feature called the Murray formation.*

   O D. *Curiosity's trek up the mountain will begin with an examination of the mountain's lower slopes.*

Text 2

What Is the International Space Station?

1 The International Space Station is a large spacecraft in orbit around Earth. It serves as a home where crews of astronauts and cosmonauts live. The space station is also a unique science laboratory. Several nations worked together to build and use the space station. The space station is made of parts that were assembled in space by astronauts. It orbits Earth at an average altitude of 220 miles. It travels at 17,500 mph. This means it orbits Earth every 90 minutes. NASA is using the space station to learn more about living and working in space. These lessons will make it possible to send humans farther into space than ever before.

How Old Is the Space Station?

2 The first piece of the International Space Station was launched in November 1998. A Russian rocket launched the Russian Zarya (zar EE uh) control module. About two weeks later, the space shuttle Endeavour met Zarya in orbit. The space shuttle was carrying the U.S. Unity node. The crew attached the Unity node to Zarya. More pieces were added over the next two years before the station was ready for people to live there. The first crew arrived in October 2000. People have lived on the space station ever since. More pieces have been added over time. NASA and its partners from around the world completed construction of the space station in 2011.

How Big Is the Space Station?

3 The space station has the volume of a five-bedroom house or two Boeing 747 jetliners. It is able to support a crew of six people, plus visitors. On Earth, the space station would weigh almost a million pounds. Measured from the edges of its solar arrays, the station covers the area of a football field including the end zones. It includes laboratory modules from the United States, Russia, Japan, and Europe.

What Are the Parts of the Space Station?

4 In addition to the laboratories where astronauts conduct science research, the space station has many other parts. The first Russian modules included basic systems needed for the space station to function. They also provided living areas for crew members. Modules called "nodes" connect parts of the station to each other.

5 Stretching out to the sides of the space station are the solar arrays. These arrays collect energy from the sun to provide electrical power. The arrays are connected to the station with a long **truss**. On the truss are radiators that control the space station's temperature.

6 Robotic arms are mounted outside the space station. The robot arms were used to help build the space station. Those arms also can move astronauts around when they go on spacewalks outside. Other arms operate science experiments.

7 Astronauts can go on spacewalks through **airlocks** that open to the outside. Docking ports allow other spacecraft to connect to the space station. New crews and visitors arrive through the ports. Astronauts fly to the space station on the Russian Soyuz. Robotic spacecraft use the docking ports to deliver supplies.

Why Is the Space Station Important?

8 The space station has made it possible for people to have an ongoing presence in space. Human beings have been living in space every day since the first crew arrived. The space station's laboratories allow crew members to do research that could not be done anywhere else. This scientific research benefits people on Earth. Space research is even used in everyday life. The results are products called "spinoffs." Scientists also study what happens to the body when people live in **microgravity** for a long time. NASA and its partners have learned how to keep a spacecraft working well. All of these lessons will be important for future space exploration.

9 NASA currently is working on a plan to explore other worlds. The space station is one of the first steps. NASA will use lessons learned on the space station to prepare for human missions that reach farther into space than ever before.

http://www.nasa.gov/audience/forstudents/5-8/features/what-is-the-iss-58.html-VBdupkvQC-U

1. If the space station were on Earth, what would be the best place for it to be located?

○ A. Downtown New York City

○ B. On a farm

○ C. In the yard of a neighborhood of houses

○ D. In an apartment

2. Which sentence from the text best helps you choose your answer from number 1?

○ A. *The space station has the volume of a five-bedroom house or two Boeing 747 jetliners.*

○ B. *The space station is also a unique science laboratory.*

○ C. *NASA is using the space station to learn more about living and working in space.*

○ D. *Docking ports allow other spacecraft to connect to the space station.*

3. According to the article, what is the ultimate goal for the space station?

○ A. For non-astronauts to live in space

○ B. To travel farther into space

○ C. For different countries to work together

○ D. To study Earth from space

Text 3

Hubble Space Telescope

1 From the dawn of humankind to a mere 400 years ago, all that we knew about our universe came through observations with the naked eye. Then Galileo turned his telescope toward the heavens in 1610. The world was in for an awakening.

2 Saturn, we learned, had rings. Jupiter had moons. That nebulous patch across the center of the sky called the Milky Way was not a cloud but a collection of countless stars. Within but a few years, our notion of the natural world would be forever changed. A scientific and societal revolution quickly ensued.

3 In the centuries that followed, telescopes grew in size and complexity and, of course, power. They were placed far from city lights and as far above the haze of the atmosphere as possible. Edwin Hubble, for whom the Hubble Telescope is named, used the largest telescope of his day in the 1920s at the Mt. Wilson Observatory near Pasadena, Calif., to discover galaxies beyond our own.

4 Hubble, the observatory, is the first major optical telescope to be placed in space, the ultimate mountaintop. Above the distortion of the atmosphere, far far above rain clouds and light pollution, Hubble has an unobstructed view of the universe. Scientists have used Hubble to observe the most distant stars and galaxies as well as the planets in our solar system.

5 Hubble's launch and deployment in April 1990 marked the most significant advance in astronomy since Galileo's telescope. Our view of the universe and our place within it has never been the same.

http://www.nasa.gov/mission_pages/hubble/story/#.VDG3nL7QC-U

1. Why is space the best place to have a telescope?

- O A. Nothing can obstruct the telescope's view.
- O B. It is not in anyone's way on Earth.
- O C. It is too heavy to be on Earth.
- O D. Any country can use the telescope.

2. What sentence best supports the answer to question 1?

- O A. *In the centuries that follow, telescopes grew in size and complexity and, of course, power.*
- O B. *Above the distortion of the atmosphere, far far above rain clouds and light pollution, Hubble has an unobstructed view of the universe.*
- O C. *Our view of the universe and our place within it has never been the same.*
- O D. *Scientists have used Hubble to observe the most distant stars and galaxies as well as the planets in our solar system.*

3. What could the word <u>nebulous</u> mean in the article?

- O A. Cloudy
- O B. Clear
- O C. Space
- O D. Telescope

Writing Task

You have read three articles about different ways that astronauts and scientists are exploring outer space. Write an essay that shows how astronauts and scientists are exploring outer space. Use information from all three articles in your essay to support your response.

Part 3: Narrative Writing

Directions: Read the selection "Thank You Ma'am" by Langston Hughes and answer the questions that follow. You will have about 50 minutes to complete this task. You may use additional time if needed.

Thank You Ma'am

Langston Hughes

1 She was a large woman with a large purse that had everything in it but hammer and nails. It had a long strap, and she carried it slung across her shoulder. It was about eleven o'clock at night, and she was walking alone, when a boy ran up behind her and tried to snatch her purse. The strap broke with the single tug the boy gave it from behind. But the boy's weight and the weight of the purse combined caused him to lose his balance so, instead of taking off full blast as he had hoped, the boy fell on his back on the sidewalk, and his legs flew up. The large woman simply turned around and kicked him right square in his blue-jeaned sitter. Then she reached down, picked the boy up by his shirt front, and shook him until his teeth rattled.

2 After that the woman said, "Pick up my pocketbook, boy, and give it here." She still held him. But she bent down enough to permit him to stoop and pick up her purse. Then she said, "Now ain't you ashamed of yourself?"

3 Firmly gripped by his shirt front, the boy said, "Yes'm." The woman said, "What did you want to do it for?" The boy said, "I didn't aim to."

4 She said, "You a lie!"

5 By that time two or three people passed, stopped, turned to look, and some stood watching. "If I turn you loose, will you run?" asked the woman.

6 "Yes'm," said the boy.

7 "Then I won't turn you loose," said the woman. She did not release him.

8 "I'm very sorry, lady, I'm sorry," whispered the boy.

9 "Um-hum! And your face is dirty. I got a great mind to wash your face for you. Ain't you got nobody home to tell you to wash your face?"

10 "No'm," said the boy.

11 "Then it will get washed this evening," said the large woman starting up the street, dragging the frightened boy behind her.

12 He looked as if he were fourteen or fifteen, frail and willow-wild, in tennis shoes and blue jeans.

13 The woman said, "You ought to be my son. I would teach you right from wrong. Least I can do right now is to wash your face. Are you hungry?"

14 "No'm," said the being dragged boy. "I just want you to turn me loose." "Was I bothering you when I turned that corner?" asked the woman.

15 "No'm."

16 "But you put yourself in contact with me," said the woman. "If you think that that contact is not going to last awhile, you got another thought coming. When I get through with you, sir, you are going to remember Mrs. Luella Bates Washington Jones."

17 Sweat popped out on the boy's face and he began to struggle. Mrs. Jones stopped, jerked him around in front of her, put a half-nelson about his neck, and continued to drag him up the street. When she got to her door, she dragged the boy inside, down a hall, and into a large kitchenette-furnished room at the rear of the house. She switched on the light and left the door open. The boy could hear other roomers laughing and talking in the large house. Some of their

doors were open, too, so he knew he and the woman were not alone. The woman still had him by the neck in the middle of her room.

18 She said, "What is your name?"

19 "Roger," answered the boy.

20 "Then, Roger, you go to that sink and wash your face," said the woman, whereupon she turned him loose—at last. Roger looked at the door—looked at the woman—looked at the door—and went to the sink.

21 "Let the water run until it gets warm," she said. "Here's a clean towel."

22 "You gonna take me to jail?" asked the boy, bending over the sink.

23 "Not with that face, I would not take you nowhere," said the woman. "Here I am trying to get home to cook me a bite to eat and you snatch my pocketbook! Maybe, you ain't been to your supper either, late as it be. Have you?"

24 "There's nobody home at my house," said the boy.

25 "Then we'll eat," said the woman, "I believe you're hungry—or been hungry—to try to snatch my pocketbook."

26 "I wanted a pair of blue suede shoes," said the boy.

27 "Well, you didn't have to snatch my pocketbook to get some suede shoes," said Mrs. Luella Bates Washington Jones. "You could of asked me."

28 "M'am?"

29 The water dripping from his face, the boy looked at her. There was a long pause. A very long pause. After he had dried his face and not knowing what else to do dried it again, the boy turned around, wondering what next. The door was open. He could make a dash for it down the hall. He could run, run, run, run, run!

30 The woman was sitting on the day-bed. After a while she said, "I were young once and I wanted things I could not get."

31 There was another long pause. The boy's mouth opened. Then he frowned, but not knowing he frowned.

32 The woman said, "Um-hum! You thought I was going to say but, didn't you? You thought I was going to say, but I didn't snatch people's pocketbooks. Well, I wasn't going to say that." Pause. Silence. "I have done things, too, which I would not tell you, son—neither tell God, if he didn't already know. So you set down while I fix us something to eat. You might run that comb through your hair so you will look presentable."

33 In another corner of the room behind a screen was a gas plate and an icebox. Mrs. Jones got up and went behind the screen. The woman did not watch the boy to see if he was going to run now, nor did she watch her purse which she left behind her on the day-bed. But the boy took care to sit on the far side of the room where he thought she could easily see him out of the corner of her eye, if she wanted to. He did not trust the woman not to trust him. And he did not want to be mistrusted now.

34 "Do you need somebody to go to the store," asked the boy, "maybe to get some milk or something?"

35 "Don't believe I do," said the woman, "unless you just want sweet milk yourself. I was going to make cocoa out of this canned milk I got here."

36 "That will be fine," said the boy.

37 She heated some lima beans and ham she had in the icebox, made the cocoa, and set the table. The woman did not ask the boy anything about where he lived, or his folks, or anything else that would embarrass him. Instead, as they ate, she told him about her job in a hotel beauty-shop that stayed open late, what the work was like, and how all kinds of women came in and out, blondes, red-heads, and Spanish. Then she cut him a half of her ten-cent cake.

38 "Eat some more, son," she said.

39 When they were finished eating she got up and said, "Now, here, take this ten dollars and buy yourself some blue suede shoes. And next time, do not make the mistake of latching onto my pocketbook nor nobody else's—because shoes come by devilish like that will burn your feet. I got to get my rest now. But I wish you would behave yourself, son, from here on in."

40 She led him down the hall to the front door and opened it. "Good-night! Behave yourself, boy!" she said, looking out into the street.

41 The boy wanted to say something else other than "Thank you, m'am" to Mrs. Luella Bates Washington Jones, but he couldn't do so as he turned at the barren stoop and looked back at the large woman in the door. He barely managed to say "Thank you" before she shut the door. And he never saw her again.

1. Part A. How many people live with Mrs. Luella Bates Washington Jones?

○ A. She lives alone.

○ B. One person

○ C. Many people

○ D. It is impossible to say.

Part B. Which statement from the story best supports your answer in Part A?

○ A. *The boy could hear other roomers laughing and talking in the large house.*

○ B. *She switched on the light and left the door open.*

○ C. *When she got to her door, she dragged the boy inside, down a hall, and into a large kitchenette-furnished room at the rear of the house.*

○ D. *In another corner of the room behind a screen was a gas plate and an icebox.*

2. **Part A.** Why didn't Mrs. Jones turn Roger in?

- ○ A. She decided to give him a second chance.
- ○ B. He didn't do anything wrong.
- ○ C. She knows his parents.
- ○ D. She made mistakes in her past.

Part B. What line from the story confirms your answer?

- ○ A. *After a while she said, "I were young once and I wanted things I could not get."*
- ○ B. *"There's nobody home at my house," said the boy.*
- ○ C. *The door was open. He could make a dash for it down the hall.*
- ○ D. *The woman still had him by the neck in the middle of her room.*

3. Put the events from the story in order. Place a number from 1 to 6 with 1 being the earliest event.

_____ Woman walks home alone at night.

_____ She gives him money for shoes.

_____ Woman takes the boy to her house.

_____ Boy tries to steal her purse.

_____ They eat supper together.

_____ Roger never sees Mrs. Jones again.

4. **Part A.** How much do the blue suede shoes cost?

- A. $2.00
- B. $20.00
- C. $5.00
- D. $10.00

Part B. This story was written more than 70 years ago. How much would those shoes most likely sell for today?

- A. $10.00
- B. $1,000.00
- C. $100.00
- D. $15.00

5. What is the best lesson that could be learned from this story?

- A. Everyone needs help once in a while.
- B. Do not steal from others.
- C. Don't walk alone at night.
- D. Sharing food is a good way to make friends.

6. How are Mrs. Jones and Roger alike?

- A. Both work at night.
- B. Both have made mistakes during their lives.
- C. Both are lonely.
- D. Both B and C.

Writing Task

Retell the story of "Thank You Ma'am" from the perspective of either Roger or Mrs. Luella Bates Washington. Consider how the story would be different.

PRACTICE TEST 2
End-of-Year Assessment (EOY)

Task 1: Informational Text

Directions: Read the following text and answer the questions that follow. You will have about 70 minutes to complete this task. You may use additional time if needed.

History of LEGO®

Excerpt from *Brick Wonders Ancient, Modern and Natural Wonders Made from LEGO*

by Warren Elsmore

1 The story began in 1916 when Ole Kirk Christiansen started a woodworking business in Billund, Denmark. He made wooden toys at first, and by the 1930s, had dubbed the company "LEGO" after an abbreviation of the Danish phrase that means, "play well." The company moved into plastics in 1947, and in 1949, they began producing plastic interlocking bricks under the name "Automatic Binding Bricks."

2 The early designs were not quite the bricks we know today, but in 1954, Ole Kirk's son, Godtfred, conceived that with the addition of doors and windows, LEGO bricks (so named in 1953) had almost limitless creative potential. The first town-plan system was released soon after, but LEGO bricks were still not the company's core business. The stud-and-tube interlocking system was developed and patented in 1958, and bricks from this date are still compatible with the ones for sale today—the most important innovation was that when they were snapped together, they remained in place. That was the year Ole Kirk died, and the business passed to Godtfred. In 1960, a warehouse fire destroyed much of the remaining stock of wooden toys, and production of them was discontinued. The company was now comprised of more than 400 employees and poised to enter the United States, Canada, and Italy. Within a few years, it spread to a host of other countries, including Finland, the Netherlands, Hong

Kong, Australia, Morocco, and Japan. The LEGO® invasion had begun.

3 By 1966, the toys were in 42 countries, and the first LEGO train had been introduced, running on a four and a half-volt motor. This was also the year that the first LEGOLAND Park was opened, in Billund, Denmark, receiving 3,000 visitors on its first day.

4 Sets have continued to be released on many different themes, from spacecrafts to pirate ships, and many technical elements have been incorporated, such as motors, magnets, and sensors. LEGO Duplo—larger bricks for younger children—were released in 1977, and the following year, miniature figurines (minifigs) followed, allowing humanoid shapes to inhabit the LEGO landscapes for the first time.

5 LEGO has inspired many people to accomplish extraordinary feats over the years, and encouraged so much energetic innovation that few records set for LEGO creations last very long. One which has lasted (so far) is the largest LEGO structure, a statue of the Sitting Bull at LEGOLAND, Denmark, which stands at almost 25 feet tall (7.75 meters) and was made from one and a half million bricks. At the time of writing, the tallest LEGO tower is a staggering 112 feet, eleven inches (32.5 meters), constructed by Red Clay Consolidated School, Wilmington.

6 I'm also proud to have my own little piece of record history. In 2012 at my LEGO Show, the largest mosaic in the world was constructed—1,549 square feet and three square inches (144 square meters), meaning that I'm the happy owner of a Guinness World Record certificate. Since then, though, the record has already been beaten at least twice. Such is the fervor and dedication of LEGO builders; these records really don't last long.

Sorting and Storing

7 There is one <u>perennial</u> problem when it comes to LEGO® bricks—sorting them. Unless you have a very small collection, it soon becomes apparent that trying to find the right LEGO element

can take more time than actually building the model. So, what to do? What is the best way of sorting your bricks?

8 If you have a very small collection—perhaps only one or two sets—then the obvious way to sort your LEGO is to not sort it at all. With not many bricks to choose between, storing all the bricks in one box is an appealing thought. Having said that, though, even if you have a large amount of LEGO, there is a benefit to this approach. Although I build in a studio, with huge numbers of bricks available in every color, sometimes my most creative builds come from using only a small number of parts. Or building from a mixed pile of LEGO—taking inspiration from the parts available at hand. Not sorting your LEGO can actually help sometimes.

9 As your LEGO collection grows, however, most people will choose to sort their LEGO so it's easier to store and build from. There are lots of ways to do this, but the most common methods chosen are either by color or by brick. Sorting by color is often the first way that LEGO fans decide to arrange their bricks. If you want to make a white house, then surely it's easier to build from a box of white bricks?

10 Sorting by color has one distinct disadvantage, though—black. Sorting through a box of black bricks is very difficult unless you have very bright lights. Black parts all seem to combine together so that you can never find the part you're looking for. As your collection grows, you'll also start to find that sorting by color becomes unmanageable. When you have one very large box of blue, how can you find that one blue 1x2 Brick with Studs on Both Sides that you need?

11 Progressing from sorting by color, many fans then sort by type. Each different element has its own drawer or box, so it's easy to find a part. As your collection grows, you realize that perhaps every part having a drawer isn't so practical—you would need tens of thousands of drawers. So, elements are grouped together—all the LEGOTechnic elements are stored together, perhaps, or all the tiles. Sorting by part works well for most medium-sized collections.

12 When you progress into "Master Builder" territory, or build professionally for a living like I do, then you need an approach that scales well. My studio contains many hundreds of thousands of bricks—almost certainly millions although I've never counted. Professional builders mainly choose to sort by both part AND color. This means that it's easy to find one exact piece, but we can also quickly get hold of, for instance, all the gray bricks.

13 Each builder will have their own system that works for them the best. In fact, I actually have two systems running concurrently in my studio.

14 When I'm planning a build, what's most important to me is the way that the bricks connect. So inside my office, the walls are surrounded by hundreds of small drawers—the same drawers that are used for storing screws. In these drawers, I keep elements by part, regardless of color. This means that if I want to check how one brick connects to another, I can quickly find the parts and check. Color isn't important to me here, as I'm usually prototyping a design to check if something will work correctly.

15 However, when I'm building a large model, such as the ones in *Brick Wonders*, it's important that I have the right shape and color of bricks. So this is where my main stores come into play. I store my bricks by part and by color. At the moment, my primary sort is by color, so I have a green section, a blue section, etc. Then within each section, I have a number of drawers, and within each drawer are the parts themselves. To make sure that the parts don't mix together, I store each part/color combination in a resealable bag.

16 So, if I'm building a small, quick model, I have everything at hand from my chair. If I'm building a large model, I can select the bags of parts that I need—or perhaps even remove entire drawers if I know I'll need, for instance, lots of white bricks.

17 There's only one real problem with having a well-sorted and stored LEGO collection. You do, of course, have to sort the bricks first!

1. Why is the name LEGO an appropriate name for the company?
   - ○ A. It means "toy" in Danish.
   - ○ B. It means "child" in Danish.
   - ○ C. It means "play well" in Danish.
   - ○ D. It means "build" in Danish.

2. What tragic event may have helped LEGO become more successful?
   - ○ A. A factory fire that destroyed the remaining wooden products
   - ○ B. A flood that washed away the factory
   - ○ C. A car accident that injured the owner of the company
   - ○ D. A factory accident that injured the employee who built the wooden toys

3. What proof does the author provide that shows how LEGO was growing in popularity in 1960?
   - ○ A. There were commercials on television.
   - ○ B. LEGOs were sold in countries all over the world.
   - ○ C. The President of the United States had LEGOs.
   - ○ D. It was the number one selling toy in the world.

4. At what point should you begin sorting your LEGOs?
   - ○ A. Every time you buy a new set.
   - ○ B. After you have your own LEGO studio.
   - ○ C. After your collection grows beyond a few sets.
   - ○ D. Only after you collect enough black LEGO pieces.

5. According to the author, if all of your black LEGO bricks are sorted together, what is the most important thing to have as you look for a specific piece?
   - ○ A. Patience
   - ○ B. Bright light
   - ○ C. Drawer space
   - ○ D. A LEGO studio

6. What is the main idea of the article?

- O A. LEGO is known around the world.
- O B. LEGO has a long history, and keeping your own LEGOs organized is important.
- O C. LEGOs are a fun toy for all ages.
- O D. LEGOs are best if sorted properly.

7. Using clues from the reading, what does the word perennial in paragraph 7 line 1 mean?

- O A. Happening constantly
- O B. Happening once a year
- O C. Happening twice a year
- O D. Happening once a month

8. If you were collecting LEGOs, what would be the best way to store them?

- O A. By color
- O B. By type
- O C. By size
- O D. It is a personal preference.

Task 2: Narrative Text

Directions: Read the following story and answer the questions that follow. You will have about 70 minutes to complete this task. You may use additional time if needed.

Cameron's Dilemma

1 Cameron's backpack was a mess as usual. He wondered how all of his papers ended up looking like they had been part of a huge paper snowball fight and then shoved back in his bag. He could never remember putting them in like that. It always annoyed Mrs. DeMarco that his homework always looked like that, even though it was always done. Cameron tried to sort through what he would need for class that day and what could wait until tonight to organize. If he didn't get moving, he was going to be late.

2 Rushing into the classroom, Cameron almost knocked down his best friend Lucas.

3 "Hey, watch it!" Kyle yelled as he jumped out of the way.

4 "Sorry, all of my homework is a mess again. I wanted to fix it before class started," Cameron said.

5 "I don't know how you do it, Cam," Kyle chuckled as he entered the room.

6 Cameron quickly moved between a couple of classmates as he tried to get to his desk and get ready for class. But before he could slide into his seat, he heard the words every student dreads.

7 "Cameron, could you come up here for a second?" asked Mrs. DeMarco.

8 Gulp. Cameron was scared to death of those words. He rarely was in trouble, but he always worried about those words. He tried to get up, but his legs weighed about 1,000 pounds. He had to use both arms to push his weight out of the chair. He stumbled up to the desk.

9 "Uh, yes Mrs. DeMarco?" stammered Cameron.

10 "I just wanted to ask you to stay behind for a minute when everyone goes to gym after class," requested Mrs. DeMarco.

11 "Okay. Sure. You got it," answered Cameron.

12 Cameron's legs weighed even more now than before. Had he done something so horrible that Mrs. DeMarco couldn't even speak about it in front of other students? He did not think so. Did his mother call and mention that Cameron was tormenting his little sister at home by hiding her new dolls so she thought they were lost? No, why would his mother do that? Oh this was going to be torture. Cameron was so upset that he didn't even notice that he walked right past his seat.

13 "I think you missed something," Kyle said as he snapped Cameron out of his trance.

14 "Oh. Thanks, Kyle," Cameron whispered.

15 "Are you okay? You look like you've seen a ghost," Kyle said.

16 "Mrs. DeMarco needs to see me after class. What could she want? She only does that when kids are really bad," Cameron wondered.

17 "Good luck, buddy. Glad it's not me!" Kyle laughed.

18 Cameron slumped into his seat and spent the next 40 minutes thinking of every possible thing he could have done wrong and why Mrs. DeMarco would want to talk to him. Sweat ran down his back, and he felt light-headed. He wondered if he passed out and went to the nurse if Mrs. DeMarco would forget.

19 Mrs. DeMarco's voice snapped Cameron out of his spell. "Okay, class, I'll see you when you get back from gym. Don't forget we have a math test when you come back."

20 The class groaned as they walked out. Cameron thought about making a break for it, but his size fives felt like they were locked in cement blocks. He may as well get it over with.

21 "Mrs. DeMarco, you wanted to see me?" Cameron asked.

22 "Oh, I almost forgot. Do you remember a few weeks ago when we wrote those poems for the Veteran's Day contest? I received a letter this morning telling me you won first prize! Congratulations! You are going to read your poem to the whole school at the assembly next week. I know you don't like speaking in front of people, so I wanted to tell you first. I didn't want to announce it to the class and make you nervous," Mrs. DeMarco explained.

23 A contest? Cameron could not believe it. He never thought about anything good. A smile broke out on his face.

24 "Cameron, do you feel all right? You looked pale during class." Mrs. DeMarco inquired.

25 "I'm fine. Thanks, Mrs. DeMarco. I just have to remember not to jump to conclusions," Cameron answered.

26 Cameron hurried out of class to catch up to Kyle. He could not wait to tell him about this!

1. What type of figurative language is the phrase "his legs weighed about 1,000 pounds"?
   - O A. Simile
   - O B. Onomatopoeia
   - O C. Hyperbole
   - O D. Personification

2. What type of figurative language is the word "Gulp"?
   - O A. Simile
   - O B. Onomatopoeia
   - O C. Hyperbole
   - O D. Personification

3. What is the lesson learned by Cameron in the story?
   - O A. Stay out of trouble.
   - O B. Don't jump to conclusions.
   - O C. Always respect your teacher.
   - O D. Treat your siblings well.

4. The author wrote, "Cameron thought about making a break for it, but his size fives felt like they were locked in cement blocks." What are his size fives?
   - O A. His pencils
   - O B. His notebooks
   - O C. His shoes
   - O D. His fingers

5. What technique does the author use to make the story seem like it really happened?
   - O A. Dialogue
   - O B. Paragraphs
   - O C. Strong descriptions
   - O D. Both A and C

Answers to Practice Tests

Practice Test 1: Performance-Based Assessment

Part 1: Literary Analysis Task

Black Beauty

1. Part A. **A** Coaxing means using gentle persuasion, so the correct answer is A.

   Part B. At least I thought so; but I knew my mother always wore one when she went out, and all horses did when they were grown up; and so, what with the nice oats, and what with my master's pats, kind words, and gentle ways, I got to wear my bit and bridle.

2. Part A. **D** The narrator mentions having a bit placed in his mouth and having iron shoes nailed to his feet, which gives the reader more information that a horse is telling the story.

   Part B. **A and B.** Both choices A and B give information that informs the reader that something other than a human is telling the story. Choices C and D could both be spoken by a person.

3. Part A. **C** Based on information from the passage, the master did not leave Black Beauty when he had his first shoes put on. This shows that the master cares for Black Beauty.

   Part B. **D** Both Choices A and B give the reader information that the master cares for Black Beauty.

4. Part A. **A** The correct answer would be A since shoes that people wear are not made of iron and attached by nails. B would not be a correct choice since the text states that the shoes were made of iron, not silver.

   Part B. **B** Roller skates are attached to the feet but not with nails. They would be the closest to horseshoes.

5. Part A. **D** Squire Gordon is looking for a horse. He visits and inspects Black Beauty and says that the horse will do well.

   Part B. He seemed to like me, and said, "When he has been well broken in he will do very well."

6. Part A. **B** Black Beauty states that he feels proud when he carries the master.

   Part B. **B** It is in this paragraph that Black Beauty states that he feels proud to carry the master.

The Secret Garden

1. Part A. **C** The author writes that Mary's mother left her alone when she was very young, which helps inform the reader that she lost her parents at a very young age.

   Part B. *If she had been older she would no doubt have been very anxious at being left alone in the world, but she was very young, and as she had always been taken care of, she supposed she always would be.*

2. Part A. **A** Self-absorbed means to be preoccupied with one's thoughts or feelings, which is another way of saying selfish.

   Part B. **A** *she gave her entire thought to herself.*

3. Part A. **B** Mistress Mary quite contrary is part of the nursery rhyme that the other children sing to Mary.

   Part B. **B** **Mistress Mary is a takeoff on** a popular children's nursery rhyme, "Mary, Mary, Quite Contrary."

4. Part A. **D** Dreary is a synonym for desolate.

   Part B. **A** An abandoned amusement park would also be desolate because it would be rundown, dreary, and quiet.

5. Part A. **D** The other three words are listed by Basil when he describes Archibald Craven.

   Part B. **B** Hunchback is a physical condition. All of the others are character traits.

6. Part A. **C** As stated in Part B, Mrs. Crawford is not fond of Mary. She pities her and does not say nice things about Mary.

   Part B. *"She is such a plain child," Mrs. Crawford said pityingly, afterward. "And her mother was such a pretty creature. She had a very pretty manner, too, and Mary has the most unattractive ways I ever saw in a child. The children call her `Mistress Mary Quite Contrary,' and though it's naughty of them, one can't help understanding it."*

Writing Task: Possible Answer

Authors use different narrators to tell their stories so that the reader is interested and wants to read more. There are different types of narrators. The main character can tell the story, which is first person. A narrator who is watching the story can tell what the characters are thinking and feeling. In *Black Beauty* and *The Secret Garden*, the authors write stories using two different narrators and that gives the reader a chance to enjoy the novels in different ways.

In *Black Beauty*, the narrator is the horse. That's right, the horse! Even though horses cannot talk in real life, Anna Sewell, the author, is able to pretend that the horse can think. This gives the reader a chance to think like a horse and imagine what he is thinking and feeling. Sewell wrote, "Every one may not know what breaking in is, therefore I will describe it. It means to teach a horse to wear a saddle and bridle, and to carry on his back a man, woman or child; to go just the way they wish, and to go quietly." Thinking what it must be like to have someone riding on your back with a saddle is something people have not experienced. By writing the book from the horse's point of view, every reader learns something they never learned before.

In *The Secret Garden*, Frances Hodgson Burnett does not choose a main character to be the narrator. She also does not choose an animal. The narrator is the narrator. A person not involved in the story is telling the story. This means that you can learn about characters from the point of view of someone who is not mad or happy or sad about what is happening in the story. You can learn the feelings and thoughts of the characters as they happen in the story. Burnett wrote, "Mary had liked to look at her mother from a distance and she had thought her very pretty, but as she knew very little of her she could scarcely have been expected to love her or to miss her very much when she was gone. She did not miss her at all, in fact, and as she was a self-absorbed child she gave her entire thought to herself, as she had always done." This shows us how Mary feels about her mom dying and that she really didn't miss her.

Writers tell great stories. When they write stories, they pick characters to tell their stories. Readers learn a lot from the narrators in the story. In *Black Beauty*, a horse tells the story, and in *The Secret Garden*, a narrator outside the story tells the story. Both ways help us enjoy the story and learn things we never knew before. That is what makes a great story.

Explanation

This essay effectively uses both stories to show why the narrator is an important part of the story. Quotes are used from both stories to prove the writer's point. This essay would receive a top score. How did you do? Did you use quotes? Did you explain how the narrator impacts the story? Look back at your essay to see if there are areas you could improve.

Part 2: Research Task

NASA's Mars Curiosity Rover Arrives at Martian Mountain

1. **D** Terrain, lakebed, and crater are geographical terms that are used on Earth and also visual descriptions so the reader can form a better picture while reading.
2. ***C*** In paragraph 9, the author writes that the rover's wheels were being damaged on the rocky terrain so the team moved the rover to a safer location.
3. **A** The Mars Exploration Rover Project is one element of NASA's ongoing preparation for a human mission to the Red Planet in the 2030s.

What Is the International Space Station?

1. **B** The space station is the size of two Boeing 747 jetliners. A farm has the most room to fit the space station.
2. **A** *The space station has the volume of a five-bedroom house or two Boeing 747 jetliners.*
3. **B** The final paragraph of the article specifically states that NASA would like to travel farther into space.

Hubble Telescope

1. **A** Nothing can obstruct the telescope's view. Paragraph 3 states the telescopes work best out of the haze of our atmosphere.
2. **B** *Above the distortion of the atmosphere, far far above the rain clouds and light pollution, Hubble has an unobstructed view of the universe.* This sentence is in paragraph 4.
3. **A** A definition for nebulous is cloudy or cloud-like. Another clue in the reading in paragraph 2 states that the nebulous patch is the Milky Way.

Writing Task: Possible Answer

Most children look up at the sky at night and wonder what it would be like to travel on a rocket ship through space. They might wonder what it would be like to visit aliens from another galaxy. A few people, astronauts and scientists, have the chance to keep their dream alive and build items to explore outer space in different ways. The Mars Rover, the Hubble telescope, and the International Space Station are three man-made inventions that are helping people on Earth learn more about space and keep the dream alive that people could explore other planets.

Each instrument used to explore outer space gives scientists a different way of learning about the galaxy we live in. The first type is the Mars Rover. This vehicle drives around the planet Mars without people on it. It is a really expensive remote control car. The Rover drives around Mars looking for areas of the planet to study to see if anyone or anything ever lived on Mars. The text states, "After landing inside Gale Crater in August 2012, Curiosity fulfilled in its first year of operations its major science goal of determining whether Mars ever offered environmental conditions favorable for microbial life. Clay-bearing sedimentary rocks on the crater floor, in an area called Yellowknife Bay, yielded evidence of a lakebed environment billions of years ago that offered fresh water, all of the key elemental ingredients for life, and a chemical source of energy for microbes." It is important to know if other planets ever had life on them. Knowing that tiny things like microbes could have lived on Mars lets us know that Earth is not the only planet that had living things on it.

The International Space Station is another man-made creation that helps us learn about space. This one floats in space and has people living on it. This way we can learn how people live in outer space and if we can do work there. The article states, "Human beings have been living in space every day since the first crew arrived. The space station's laboratories allow crew members to do research that could not be done anywhere else. This scientific research benefits people on Earth. Space research is even used in everyday life. The results are products called "spinoffs." By having people working in outer space, scientists are able to learn more about the effects and if we can travel farther away from Earth one day.

Another invention that is floating in space but without people on it is the Hubble telescope. This is different than the telescopes we use on Earth because it floats in outer space and can see farther than a normal telescope. The article states, "Above the distortion of the atmosphere, far far above rain clouds and light pollution, Hubble has an unobstructed view of the universe. Scientists have used Hubble to observe the most distant stars and galaxies as well as the planets in our solar system." It has given people a chance to see farther into outer space than we ever could have imagined.

The inventions of scientists and astronauts have given people on Earth the ability to keep dreaming about outer space and the chance to visit other planets. Once this was only a dream, but with the Mars Rover, International Space Station, and Hubble telescope, it is now a real possibility to travel in space.

Explanation

This essay addresses how three inventions in space are changing the way we view outer space travel. The essay quotes each article, addresses the prompt, and is clear and appropriate in all parts of the essay. The essay shows that the writer understands English and makes few errors.

How did you do on your essay? Did you plan your writing, write a strong introduction, and use all three of the texts? Read through your essay again to see if there are any areas you would change.

Part 3: Narrative Writing

"Thank You Ma'am"

1. **Part A. C** Part B illustrates a sentence from the story that shows Mrs. Jones lives in a house with many people.

   Part B. A *The boy could hear other roomers laughing and talking in the large house.*

2. **Part A. D** She made mistakes in her past. This is illustrated by the answer to Part B.

   Part B. A *After a while she said, 'I were young once and I wanted things I could not get."*

3. Woman walks home alone at night.
   Boy tries to steal her purse.
   Woman takes the boy to her house.
   They eat supper together.
   She gives him money for shoes.
   Roger never sees Mrs. Jones again.

4. **Part A. D** Roger tells Mrs. Jones that he wanted blue suede shoes, and Mrs. Jones gives Roger $10.00 at the end of the story.

   Part B. C The other answers are either too close to the original number or too high for a pair of shoes.

5. **A** Everyone needs help once in a while. A possible answer is that you should not steal, but because Mrs. Jones made mistakes in her past, she gave Roger the money. She showed that everyone needs help.

6. **D** Mrs. Jones told Roger that she had made mistakes. Both of the characters in the story are alone. Mrs. Jones lives alone in her room, and Roger says that his parents are never home.

Writing Task: Possible Answer

I need those shoes. I need those shoes. I thought the same thing over and over again. If I was ever going to impress my friends, I needed blue suede shoes. The only problem was that I didn't have the money. Mom and Dad are never around. How could I get the money?

A few seconds later, I saw an older woman was walking alone. She looked tired. I was young and fast. I could run right by her, grab her purse and be gone before she has a chance to scream.

I ran toward the woman. I reached out for her purse. I grabbed the purse, but the strap broke. I went flying and landed on the ground. The old woman kicked me right in the backside. It already hurt from landing on it, but now it hurt even more. The woman grabbed me. Wow, was she strong! I couldn't move! Now I was in trouble. I'm going to jail. Tears were in my eyes.

The woman asked me what I was doing. I panicked and told her that I didn't mean to do it. That made it worse! She called me a liar. I just wanted to run away as fast as I could, but my knees were shaking. The woman told me her name, Mrs. Luella Bates Washington Jones. Boy was that a mouthful.

Instead of taking me to jail, she took me to her house. She said my face was dirty, and she wouldn't take me to jail looking like that. I wanted to run, but I didn't want to make her mad again.

When we got to her house, she told me to wash my face. I tried to steal her purse, and she's being nicer to me than my parents. After I washed my face, we ate supper together. She told me she made mistakes when she was younger. Maybe she felt sorry for me. I felt so bad about the purse.

Mrs. Jones asked me why I wanted the purse. When I told her about the blue suede shoes. She shook her head and started telling me about her job. When we were finished, she gave me ten dollars! I couldn't believe it. I wanted to say something, but the only thing that came out of my mouth was, "Thank you, m'am." That's it. Mrs. Luella Bates Washington Jones went back inside. I never saw her again, but I never forgot her. I promised myself I would never steal again.

Explanation

This response retells the story of "Thank you M'am" from the point of view of Roger. The story does not use as many quotes as Langston Hughes, but the main parts of the story are included, and the same theme is evident. The writer understands the writing task and has a strong grasp of language. This would receive a top score.

Practice Test 2: End-of-Year Assessment

History of LEGO

1. ***C*** This answer can be found in paragraph 1.
2. **A** This answer can be found in paragraph 2.
3. **B** Paragraph 3 states, "By 1966, the toys were in 42 countries, and the first LEGO train had been introduced, running on a four and a half-volt motor."
4. ***C*** Paragraph 9 states, "As your LEGO collection grows, however, most people will choose to sort their LEGO so it's easier to store and build from."
5. **B** Bright light. It is harder to find a black brick when all of the black bricks are together.
6. **B** Each part of the article addresses different information about LEGOs, which gives the reader two main ideas.
7. **A** Perennial means lasting for an indefinitely long time.
8. **D** The author states that LEGO collectors should find the best way that works for them.

Cameron's Dilemma

1. ***C*** Hyperbole is an overexaggeration. Cameron's legs do not really weigh 1,000 pounds.
2. **B** Onomatopoeia is a word that is an imitation of a sound. Gulp is a sound turned into a word.
3. **B** Cameron is nervous that he is in trouble and it limits his ability to pay attention in class.
4. ***C*** Cameron's size fives are his shoes. He wears a size five shoe.
5. **D** Dialogue and description are necessary for an author to create a real experience for the reader.

Index

Put New Jersey Students on the Path to Success

NEW JERSEY STATE ASSESSMENT TESTS

Preparing students for success is so important. That's why these newly revised study guides are the perfect tools to help students get ready for the PARCC (The Partnership for Assessment of Readiness for College and Careers) tests in the State of New Jersey. Through a series of high quality, computer-based K–12 assessments in Mathematics and English Language Arts, teachers, schools, and parents can rest assured that students are on track for success. Each title features:

- Two full-length practice tests with answers and explanations
- In-depth review through engaging lessons, hints, and tips for each PARCC test
- Content reflective of classroom lessons and aligned to Common Core Curriculum
- An explanation and overview of the PARCC assessment

Give students the help they need to achieve their very best—now and in the future.

New Jersey Grade 3 Math Test
Thomas Walsh, M.A., M.Ed., Ed.D. and Dan Nale, M.Ed., MBA
ISBN 978-1-4380-0562-1, $12.99, *Can$14.99*

New Jersey Grade 4 ELA/Literacy Test
Kelli Eppley, M.S.
ISBN 978-1-4380-0561-4, $12.99, *Can$14.99*

New Jersey Grade 5 ELA/Literacy Test
Mark Riccardi and Kimberly Perillo
ISBN 978-1-4380-0560-7, $12.99, *Can$14.99*

Each book: Paperback, approx. 216–288 pp., 7 13/16" x 10"

Available at your local book store
or visit **www.barronseduc.com**

Barron's Educational Series, Inc.
250 Wireless Blvd.
Hauppauge, NY 11788
Order toll-free: 1-800-645-3476

In Canada: Georgetown Book Warehouse
34 Armstrong Ave.
Georgetown, Ont. L7G 4R9
Canadian orders: 1-800-247-7160

Prices subject to change without notice.

(#156) R11/14

BARRON'S